CAMBRIDGE
CHECKPOINTS
2017–2019

HSC Community and Family Studies

- Revision summaries for all core modules and most options
- Groups in Context – Mandatory A groups and two Category B groups
- Hints and tips about the CAFS HSC exam
- Sample exam questions
- Sample answers

Kelly Bell
Kate Rayner

CAMBRIDGE
UNIVERSITY PRESS

CAMBRIDGE
UNIVERSITY PRESS

University Printing House, Cambridge CB2 8BS, United Kingdom

One Liberty Plaza, 20th Floor, New York, NY 10006, USA

477 Williamstown Road, Port Melbourne, VIC 3207, Australia

4843/24, 2nd Floor, Ansari Road, Daryaganj Delhi – 110002, India

79 Anson Road, #06–04/06, Singapore 079906

Cambridge University Press is part of the University of Cambridge.

It furthers the University's mission by disseminating knowledge in the pursuit of
education, learning and research at the highest international levels of excellence.

www.cambridge.org
Information on this title: www.cambridge.org/9781316616239

First published 2016
20 19 18 17 16 15 14 13 12 11 10 9 8 7 6 5 4 3 2

Printed in Australia by Ligare Pty Ltd

*A Cataloguing-in-Publication entry is available from the catalogue
of the National Library of Australia at* www.nla.gov.au

ISBN 9781-316-61623-9 Paperback

Additional resources for this publication at www.cambridge.edu.au/hsccheckpoints

The author and publisher wish to thank the following sources for permission to reproduce material:
Images: Graph of labour force participation rates 2012 – Australian Institute of Health and Welfare;
(ABS). Creative Commons (CC) BY 3.0 licence, **p.147.**

*Every effort has been made to trace and acknowledge copyright. The publishers apologise for any accidental
infringement and welcome information that would rectify any error or omission in subsequent editions.*

Contents

Introduction

Congratulations on choosing Community and Family Studies (CAFS) as part of your pattern of study in the Higher School Certificate (HSC). We have great confidence that you will find studying this course enjoyable and challenging.

CAFS is a subject that explores a diversity of issues affecting the lives of all individuals and their unique roles in groups, families and communities. Students discover the importance of managing individual and group needs and resources to help satisfy wellbeing. In addition, CAFS allows students an opportunity to investigate a variety of groups within the community and the impact that individuals can have on the betterment of the groups, families and communities to which they belong. CAFS explores the importance of a variety of school, family and social groups; community organisations; and government agencies working together to support the needs of individuals in the community. CAFS builds on skills and knowledge in research, resource management, decision-making, goal setting, conflict resolution, communication, problem solving, leadership, relationship building, safe technology use and advocacy.

Checkpoints HSC Community and Family Studies provides students with a resource that will help support and consolidate their knowledge and understanding of CAFS in preparation for internal assessments and the NSW Board of Studies HSC CAFS examination. This resource is to be used alongside student course work, textbooks and other resources that are available to support their learning in CAFS.

In this book, students are provided with hints and tips, as well as information about the structure of the HSC CAFS examination. Chapters include brief revision summaries aligned with the NSW Board of Studies CAFS Stage 6 Syllabus amended in 2013. It includes the main concepts in each core and in the two most popular options, *Social Impact of Technology* and *Individuals and Work*. We apologise for not including *Family and Societal Interactions*, but should this option gain greater popularity we may be able to include a chapter on it in the future.

Following the summaries, past HSC and sample examination questions are presented, with answers to multiple-choice questions and suggested short answers. The second last chapter includes questions from the 2015 HSC CAFS Examination and the last chapter presents suggested answers for the 2015 HSC CAFS Examination.

In the revision summaries of each chapter, italicised words indicate an italicised sub-heading from the syllabus, bolded words are dot points from the syllabus, underlined words are dash points or examples from the syllabus, and italicised underlined words are Learn to objectives; for example, *research fundamentals,* **sampling**, <u>methods</u> and *<u>existing research projects</u>*.

It must be stressed that the suggested answers provided in this resource are not definitive and there may be other acceptable answers that are not presented. Answers have been written to provide guidance in the range of acceptable answers, not just exemplars. As previously mentioned, students should use this resource in conjunction with other resources for this subject to help them be better prepared for CAFS examinations, in particular the HSC examination.

As the format of the CAFS HSC exam was altered in 2010 and the syllabus was amended in 2013, some questions have been adapted and new ones created to reflect these changes.

Cambridge University Press and the author team would be very grateful for feedback on this resource and how it can be improved for subsequent editions.

The Cambridge QuizMe App, compatible with all internet-enabled devices, is available at www.cambridge.edu.au/hsccheckpointsapp. It features quizzes that are an extra revision tool for use throughout the year and is a fun add-on to your study experience.

We wish you all success and enjoyment in Community and Family Studies.

Good luck with the HSC course and the HSC exam!

Kelly and Kate.

Acknowledgements

We would like to thank the Board of Studies Teaching and Educational Standards (BOSTES) NSW for permission for the reproduction of the HSC CAFS examination questions included in this resource. Each question from past HSC CAFS examinations is indicated at the end of the question.

Thank you to the dedicated and hardworking CAFS teachers around New South Wales, especially those that are part of The CAFS Network, for their continual commitment and passion for the subject. You have made a difference to the lives of so many students in your care through teaching the valuable life skills and values embedded in this subject.

To the CAFS students whom we have taught over the years, your own love and enjoyment of this subject has motivated us to continue to advocate for this subject and share our passion with other teachers.

Understanding CAFS

CAFS consists of two 120-hour courses. Although the Preliminary course is not examined in the HSC, essential skills and knowledge are built throughout the three mandatory modules. This content and understanding builds the foundations for students and is embedded in the HSC course. Successful CAFS students will demonstrate a strong interconnectedness between concepts throughout their exam responses.

The HSC CAFS course comprises three core modules representative of 75 per cent of course time. Students also choose to study one option, which represents 25 per cent of course time (BOS, 2013, p. 10). All three cores and the option chosen are examined in the HSC CAFS examination.

It is important to know your CAFS syllabus intimately. Download it, print it off, colour code it, check it off, get to know the syllabus terms very well. Due to the interconnectedness of the course, it is important to note the relationship between the 'Learn about' and 'Learn to' objectives.

Knowledge and understanding of the CAFS performance descriptors, as well as the standards, are also essential in setting up students for success in CAFS. It allows them to see what is expected for each of the descriptors and what they need to achieve to receive certain results in the course.

Preparing for the HSC CAFS Examination

As with any examination (task/job/test/assessment) it is essential to be fully prepared. Students are encouraged to develop **goal setting** practices at the start of both the Preliminary and HSC course. SMART (Specific, Measurable, Achievable, Realistic and Timely) goals should be shared with the class teacher and classmates and should be displayed and reviewed throughout the course of study.

By **planning** and **organising** through labelling class notes, colour coding syllabus points, tracking syllabus Learn about and Learn to objectives and keeping up to date with classwork, students are making positive decisions in order to manage their resources in CAFS. Being organised also means having the correct equipment, eating healthy food, sleeping adequately, spending time with family and friends, as well as making time for relaxation and recreation.

Students need to **communicate** with their teacher their strengths and weaknesses in all areas of classwork. For effective preparation, students need to clarify their own understanding of class content by asking questions and seeking teacher feedback. Students should make the most of the many opportunities offered by their teachers to develop, practise and refine their skills and understanding of course content.

It is essential for students to engage in positive **decision-making**, where they can weigh up the options for themselves before making decisions. Making positive decisions for their education is important. Pre-reading texts or other sources before class is important. Watching current affair programs, keeping an eye on relevant news stories and participating in revision sessions can assist students to gain that extra edge over other students. Students also need to be able to make the right decisions in balancing their multiple commitments.

Problem-solving is essential in that students need to have the confidence and self-esteem to tackle challenges when faced with them. They must also to ask for help from teachers, parents and peers when they need it. Engaging in stress-management techniques is a positive step towards managing the anxiety and stress often related to the HSC and exams. It is important for students to be resilient and recognise that they are not alone and can seek help from informal and formal support to enhance not only their coursework, but also their overall wellbeing.

Studying for the HSC CAFS examination

While preparation for the HSC CAFS examination is essential, it is the actual studying and revising of the course work that creates successful students out of good students.

Developing a study timetable well in advance is important. Scheduling set time for CAFS (and other subjects) means that there are dedicated time periods where students can just focus on a particular subject. Adopting an assortment of studying techniques allows for variety and the development of different skill bases. Studying techniques might include but are not limited to: creating summaries using colour coding; reading through notes; creating mind maps; sketching and cartooning; using flash cards; participating in physical and online quizzes such as Quizlet and Kahoot; using game-based strategies such as Pictionary, Sale of the Century, Taboo, Celebrity Head and Jeopardy; using physical and online whiteboards; recording notes and questions in person or via voice recording; teaching peers (or even family members and pets). The ideas are limitless, as long as students are engaged and motivated by the various forms they adopt.

Some students participate in study sessions offered by their class teacher before and after school, or even in the school holidays, as a class or in small student groups. Some students may also wish to participate in HSC enrichment days, online workshops and webinars, seminars, lectures or other events offered by external organisations.

The most important studying technique that students can adopt is practising past and sample HSC questions such as the ones presented in this resource. Replicating the CAFS HSC examination protocols and procedures allows students the chance to experience what it is like to sit the examination.

Having a good understanding of the interrelationship between course concepts and the NSW Board of Studies Glossary of Key Words can be a positive move in achieving good results in CAFS. Using word banks and scaffolds is also a good strategy to adopt. Students who are able to apply their understanding through the use of explanations and examples have a better chance at expressing relevant and clear responses to exam style questions, therefore meeting the marking criteria successfully.

The Glossary of Key Words gives students an indication of how to respond to a particular question and how much to write. Lines provided and marks allocated to each question also give the students an indication of how to approach each question.

Various key words that have been used in past HSC CAFS examinations are also featured in the CAFS syllabus and performance descriptions. These include: account, analyse, apply, assess, compare, contrast, critically analyse/assess/evaluate/examine, define, describe, discuss, evaluate, examine, explain, identify, investigate, justify, outline, predict, propose and recount. These can be found at http://www.boardofstudies.nsw.edu.au/syllabus_hsc/glossary_keywords.html

Questions have also increasingly been developed using self-explanatory terms, and the NSW Board of Studies (2012) states that questions will continue to use terms such as 'how', or 'why' or 'to what extent'.

It is imperative that students are given many opportunities to practise using a variety of Glossary of Key Words and respond to exam style questions accordingly. A number of scaffolds have also been developed to assist students in this area, and students are encouraged to seek these out or ask their teachers for assistance.

In addition, students are strongly encouraged to answer a number of exam style questions under timed exam conditions with peer or teacher feedback. Students can use the questions in this resource and submit them to their teacher for marking. Students may also like to create a set of marking guidelines for questions and then peer mark responses. They are also encouraged to share success amongst the class by photocopying or sharing good responses. It is recommended that students use the Glossary of Key Words, line space and mark allocation in their preparation, as well as hand writing their responses.

Students can use the RUN FAR (Bell, 2014) approach to examination questions and the PEEL/TEEL (or similar) strategy to assist with the development of their responses.

The most important message to students is to practice, practice, practice!

Structure of an HSC CAFS response

Students who achieve good results in CAFS demonstrate the ability to write in a clear and concise manner.

The following steps can be used to approach examination style questions and their adaptation may lead to improvement and/or success in the course.

RUN FAR (Bell, 2014)

1 Read all parts of the question carefully.

2 Underline syllabus content, circle Glossary of Key Words and box common terms.

3 Note down definitions of syllabus terms or Glossary of Key Words.

4 Formulate a plan to your answer by using dot points, mind maps, diagrams, acronyms, and tables.

5 Answer the question using PEEL, using the space provided as a guide.

6 Review and read your response to ensure it completely answers the question.

PEEL/TEEL

Point – state your main point/**T**opic sentence.
e.g. *Firstly. To begin with.*

Elaborate – expand on your previous point.
e.g. *Therefore. This indicates that. This demonstrates. This means that. This concept impacts on.*

Evidence – provide evidence and specific examples in support of your main point/s.
e.g. *For example, this can be seen through. Evidence of this includes. An example of this is.*

Link – create a transition to your next point or from your last point. Include wellbeing where appropriate.
e.g. *In conclusion. This results in. Furthermore. As previously discussed. Conversely. Similarly.*

What to expect in the HSC CAFS Examination

Structure
The HSC CAFS Examination consists of two sections: Section I – Parts A and B and Section II.

Section I
Part A includes 20 multiple-choice questions worth one mark each, from all three core modules – Research Methodology; Groups in Context; and Parenting and Caring. It is suggested that students allow approximately *35 minutes* for this part.

Questions are ordered according to the level of difficulty, starting with easier questions and working up to more challenging questions.

Answers are to be indicated on a multiple-choice answer sheet.

Part B includes a series of short-answer questions worth 55 marks in total, from all three core modules – Research Methodology; Groups in Context; and Parenting and Caring. It is suggested that students allow approximately *1 hour and 45 minutes* for this part. As a guide, students should spend approximately 1.5 minutes per mark. So if a question is worth four marks, they should spend six minutes answering that question.

This section includes low order (define, describe, explain, identify, outline, how, why, to what extent) and high order questions (account, analyse, assess, compare, contrast, discuss, evaluate, examine, justify, propose, recount).

Answers are to be written in the spaces provided which offers guidance as to the expected length of the response.

Section II includes a series of low to high order questions from the three options – Family and Societal Interactions; Social Impact of Technology; and Individuals and Work. This section is worth 25 marks. It is suggested that students allow approximately *45 minutes* for this section. Students are to *answer and clearly label questions from the option they have studied in class.*

PLEASE NOTE THAT THIS TEXT COVERS TWO OF THE THREE OPTIONS ONLY: SOCIAL IMPACT OF TECHNOLOGY, AND INDIVIDUALS AND WORK.

Answers are to be clearly labelled and written in the writing booklets provided. Generally, parts are to be written in separate writing booklets.

Timing
5 minutes reading time, 3 hours working time.

Total marks allocated
100 marks

Research Methodology
This core will appear in Section I, Part A Multiple choice and Section I, Part B Short answer. Some questions in the HSC examination may be based around the Independent Research Project (IRP) process and include questions about how data is gathered. Students may need to apply their understanding of research methods in questions and may be given graphs, tables and/or statistics to interpret.

Groups in Context
Questions in this core can appear in Section I, Part A Multiple choice (Category A: People with disabilities and Homeless people). In Section I, Part B Short-answer section, the first part of the Groups in Context syllabus for People with disabilities and Homeless people can be examined, including: prevalence of each group within the community, individual diversity within each group, terminology used by the community to describe the group, satisfactions of needs, access to services and factors affecting access to services.

Students can then be examined in Section I, Part B Short answer section on the two Category B groups chosen to research in class: Aged; Culturally and Linguistically Diverse communities; Aboriginal and Torres Strait Islander peoples; Rural and remote families; Gay, Lesbian, Bisexual, Transgender and Intersex communities; Sole parents; Youth: all of the Groups in Context syllabus.

Students may be required to compare and contrast two or more groups for the first part of syllabus and may be given case studies, statistics, graphs and tables to interpret.

Parenting and Caring
Questions can appear in Section I, Part A Multiple-choice and Section I, Part B Short-answer section. Students may be given case studies, statistics, graphs and tables to interpret. It is wise for students to include examples about parents *and* carers. The common term 'impact' is used across many aspects of this core. This includes an impact on parents, carers, children and dependants. Concepts such as influence and wellbeing are also explored throughout this core.

Options: Family and Societal Interactions; Social Impact of Technology; and Individuals and Work
Students are instructed to ONLY choose the option they have studied in class and are presented with a rubric at the start of the section, which looks similar to the rubric shown below. Students will be presented with a variety of different questions for each option, all of which they are required to answer. Each question uses a different verb from the Glossary of Key Words, differs in mark allocation and ranges in level of difficulty. These responses are to be written in writing booklets, clearly marked with the question, centre and student number.

Section II
25 marks
Attempt ONE question from Questions 29–31
Allow about 45 minutes for this section

Answer parts (a) and (b) of the question in a writing booklet. Answer part (c) of the question in a SEPARATE writing booklet. Extra writing booklets are available.

In your answer you will be assessed on how well you:

- demonstrate knowledge and understanding of societal influences on wellbeing relevant to the question
- apply the skills of critical thinking and analysis
- communicate ideas and information using relevant examples
- present a logical and cohesive response.

(BOSTES, 2015)

Sitting the HSC CAFS Examination

Now that students are well prepared for the CAFS HSC exam it is time to put that practise into action.

It is essential that students get plenty of rest the night before, eat a nutritious meal and keep hydrated before (and during) the examination. They should also make sure they have the necessary writing equipment with them, a black pen (or two). To ease the stress, students should be aware of what time the examination begins and where it will be held and make all necessary arrangements to be there well in advance.

Coming into the examination room, students should practise some relaxation or stress management techniques so their minds are fresh to approach the examination. Becoming aware of the clocks in the room (or wearing a watch) and knowing the start and end times is important to keep on track.

Upon commencement of reading time, students should read the examination cover to cover and ensure that all sections appear on their table. Once the initial read is done, students can go back to the multiple-choice and other questions to start answering the questions in their heads. When time starts, students can then indicate their correct responses on the multiple-choice answer sheet provided.

Students are encouraged to approach their questions using the RUN FAR (Bell, 2014) strategy and answer the examination questions using the PEEL (or SEAL, TEEL, TEAL) writing strategy. It is essential that students use the plan they have written around the question to stay on track in their response. Students should never leave an answer blank and at least try to write something relating to the question or the course. They should come back to questions that they may be spending too much time on.

Students should ensure that their writing is legible and that they try to stick within the lines provided. If a student makes a mistake and writes something they are not 100% happy with, a suggestion is to put it in brackets so it can possibly add to their response, rather than being crossed out and remaining unmarked. Once all examination questions have been answered to the student's full potential, students are encouraged to read back over their responses and include any extra examples or additions where necessary.

Most importantly, students should show what they know, don't panic and make full use of the time and space allocated.

Where can I get extra help?

Students are strongly encouraged to seek the assistance of their class teacher or another experienced CAFS teacher at their school if they are stuck. Having open and honest conversations with their teacher is important in maintaining a good rapport.

In the second instance, students can use the range of resources available at the BOSTES website, including the syllabus document, performance descriptions, Glossary of Key Words, past examinations, marking guidelines, multiple-choice answers, sample answers and standards materials. http://www.boardofstudies.nsw.edu.au/hsc/

Other organisations may also offer support through resources, workshops, webinars, seminars and lectures. Examples include ACHPER NSW, HSC in the Holidays, Sydney University, Western Sydney University and other private organisations.

Peers, teachers and family members should also be consulted to provide informal support to students.

Chapter 1

Research Methodology

Research Methodology is a mandatory core module and should occupy approximately 25 per cent of total course time (BOS, 2013, p. 26).

The module builds upon the knowledge and skills developed in the Preliminary course around research methodologies. It is within this module that students also explore issues related to inquiry and research, including the Independent Research Project (IRP).

As stated previously, students can be examined on the content learnt *about* in this core module (as well as knowledge and skills already developed on the research methodologies explored in the Preliminary course) as well any skills that the students have learnt *to* do within the module and during the IRP process.

HSC core 1: Research Methodology

Research fundamentals

Students learn about:	Students learn to:

research methodology
research fundamentals
• the purpose of research, e.g. advance knowledge, increase understanding, educate others, inform practice
• the focus of research, e.g. question/hypothesis
• sampling
  – methods
  – sample group
  – sample size
	• explore a variety of existing research projects/reports and consider the following questions:
	  – what was the focus of the research?
	  – what was the sample group and size?
	  – what type of data was collected?
	  – what sources of data were used?

Revision summary

Research is the methodical investigation into and study of materials and sources in order to establish facts, build on existing findings or reach new conclusions.

There are various *research fundamentals* including **the purpose of research**; **the focus of research**; **sampling**; **types of data**; **sources of data**; **reliability and validity**; and **ethical behaviour**.

The **purpose of research** can vary according to the approach of the researcher, type of research conducted and the methods used. The purpose can be to **advance knowledge** where a researcher conducts research to gather information about a particular topic; to **increase understanding** if current research has already been conducted in a particular focus area; or to **inform practice** about future directions or intentions.

The **focus of research** includes what the investigation will be guided by, whether it is a question or a hypothesis.

A question in research includes a problem, which has the intention of being solved through the research being conducted, posed as a question or a statement. Alternatively, a hypothesis is a prediction statement that will be either proven or disproven through conducting the research.

Researchers will use **sampling** in their investigations to answer their focus question or to prove or disprove their hypothesis. Sampling is used to reduce time and costs, and it is a representation of the population being investigated. Researchers will have to decide on the sampling methods, sample group and sample size. Sampling methods include simple random sampling, systematic sampling, stratified sampling, cluster sampling, multi-stage sampling, quota sampling, convenience sampling and volunteer sampling.

Simple random sampling means that each individual within the population has an equal chance of inclusion in the sample. Systematic sampling means that there is a gap made between each selection from the population. Stratified sampling involves dividing the population into groups called strata then using simple random sampling or systematic sampling within each stratum. Cluster sampling divides the population into various groups or clusters. From these clusters, random clusters are chosen to represent the whole population. Multi-stage sampling involves selecting a sample from within specific chosen clusters. Quota sampling is where stratified sampling is used, but the selection is non-random. Convenience sampling involves choosing samples using no method to differentiate the population as they are accessed conveniently. Volunteer sampling involves individuals volunteering their participation in a study so no structured method is actually used.

The sample group is the representative sample that has been chosen to be the target population. The sample size is how many representatives will make up the sample group and may be dependent on the focus of the research, the purpose, sampling method, time, money and access to services.

A variety of *existing research projects/reports* can be explored and the focus of the research, sample group and size, type of data collected and sources of data used can be identified.

Sample examination questions: Multiple choice

1   **Which of the following best defines a *hypothesis*?**
(A) An explanation of a topic
(B) A set of rules of conduct to be followed in research
(C) A problem or statement to be investigated through research
(D) A process used to select individuals to participate in research
(BOS, 2013)

2   **A survey is to be conducted of the student population of a co-educational high school.**
   Which of the following will result in a random sample of students being chosen for this survey?
(A) Selecting five students from each year group
(B) Selecting students on the basis of their gender
(C) Selecting students on the basis of their postcode
(D) Selecting every fourth student as they enter the school
(BOS, 2011)

Sample examination question: Short answer

1   **Describe the purpose of research.** (3 marks)

The purpose of research is to create a hypothesis or research question which – when data is collected and analysed and conclusions are drawn – enhances the knowledge and increases the understanding of the audience on a particular topic. Research aims to educate others on the overall findings of the results, with the hope that any recommendations based on the conclusions can inform the practice of future researchers/companies or social groups.

Types of data

Students learn about:	Students learn to:

research fundamentals
• types of data
  – primary and secondary
  – qualitative and quantitative
• sources of data
  – individuals and groups
  – print and digital
	• describe the types of data that can be collected from individuals and groups
	• examine data from print and electronic sources to determine the key findings
	• discuss the advantages and limitations of each of the sources of data
	• explore a variety of existing research projects/reports and consider the following questions:
	  – what was the focus of the research?
	  – what was the sample group and size?
	  – what type of data was collected?
	  – what sources of data were used?

Revision summary

Researchers need to consider the **types of data** they are going to use in their investigations. This will include both <u>primary</u> data where research is collected through first-hand investigations conducted by the researcher and <u>secondary</u> data where research is gathered through second-hand investigations by other researchers or sources who have presented research on a particular focus area.

Researchers will use various methods to conduct primary research and these methods will use both <u>qualitative</u> and <u>quantitative</u> data.

Quantitative data are types of primary data that use numbers or statistics; for example, closed questions in questionnaires and experiments. Conversely, qualitative data encompass non-numerical data in the form of opinions, feelings, beliefs and/or attitudes; for example, case studies, observations, interviews, focus groups or open questions in questionnaires.

Using both types of data enables researchers to collect a range of views and opinions, thus contributing to the reliability and validity of their research.

Through their investigations, researchers need to also use various **sources of data**. These sources can be from <u>individuals and groups</u> as well as from <u>print and digital media</u>.

Individuals and groups refer to the people and organisations from which researchers can obtain their primary data, but also gain background secondary data for their literature review. Individuals can be contacted through personal contacts or connections, industry contacts, experts or specialists such as neighbours or doctors. Groups can be from government, non-government or community organisations such as Family and Community Services, Barnardos or The Lions Club. The types of data obtained from both individuals and groups can vary.

Print sources such as journals, textbooks, magazines, newspapers, pamphlets and resource sheets can support the findings of researchers. Digital sources, such as computer programs, the internet, search engines, television programs, radio, films, documentaries, CDs, DVDs, podcasts, reliable blogs, webcasts, video clips and e-books, can be used obtain key findings of research. Each of these sources of data has various advantages and limitations.

Sample examination questions: Multiple choice

3   **Which type of information is most likely to be collected by quantitative research methods?**
(A) Attitudes and values
(B) Non-numerical data
(C) Descriptions and explanations
(D) Measurements and statistics
(BOSTES, 2014)

4   **Which of the following are techniques for collecting data from primary sources?**
(A) Conducting interviews, accessing websites and books
(B) Making observations, accessing journal articles and magazines
(C) Conducting questionnaires and surveys, viewing documentaries
(D) Making observations, conducting questionnaires and experiments
(BOS, 2011)

5   **What is the main benefit of obtaining data through qualitative research?**
(A) It ensures confidentiality of data.
(B) It is quick and simple to interpret.
(C) Large quantities of data can be measured.
(D) Respondents provide opinions, attitudes and beliefs concerning the topic.
(BOS, 2010)

Sample examination questions: Short answer

2   **How do quantitative and qualitative methods of research differ?**
(4 marks) (BOS, 2013)

Quantitative methods are more objective and more reliable in that they use numerical data obtained from research methods such as experiments and closed questions from questionnaires and interviews. Data collection using this method is less time consuming. Qualitative methods differ because they use subjective data that come from people's opinions, values, attitudes and beliefs, which may be biased. Research methods that collect qualitative data include open-ended questions in questionnaires and interviews, observations and case studies.

3 Describe how quantitative data can be presented. (3 marks) (BOS, 2013)

As quantitative data uses numerical information, it can be presented using graphs such as pie, line, bar/column or histogram and tables with raw data, statistics or percentages.

Graphs convert number and statistical data into visual representations, making it easier to read and understand the data. Pie graphs show the relationship of parts, line graphs often display trends or changes, bar/column graphs often compare or show changes over time, and histograms compare two sets of data.

Another form of presenting quantitative data is in a table. Tables can include different variables and be used for tallying, comparing or displaying raw data. They can be used for data analysis and to help reach conclusions in research.

4 The table below shows adoptions in Australia over the last 20 years.

Approximate number of adoptions in Australia

	1991–1995	1996–2000	2001–2005	2006–2010
Children adopted from within Australia	3191	1730	969	850
Children adopted from overseas	1404	1333	1665	1587
Total adoptions in Australia	4595	3063	2634	2437

Part (a) of this question can be found in the Parenting and Caring chapter.

(b) Describe primary and secondary sources that may have been used to produce the data in the table. (6 marks) (BOS, 2012)

The primary sources that may have been used to produce the data in the table include questionnaires and/or interviews of adoptive families. Australian adoptive families could have been asked closed-ended questions before, during and after the adoption process.

It is more likely that secondary sources may have been used to produce the numerical data in the table. Data may include statistics from the Australian Bureau of Statistics. These statistics could have been obtained from the four-year census that all Australians have to participate in.

Family and Community Services or private organisations, such as Barnardos or Catholic Care, could also document statistical data of Australian and overseas adoptions. These organisations may have been contacted through interviews (primary) to provide information to produce the data in the table. Other sources that could have been accessed are research studies or journal articles on adoption in Australia, which could have also been used to produce the data in the table. These would be of particular importance if studies were conducted over a long period.

5   **Outline the advantages and disadvantages of gathering data for research from both print sources and from individuals/groups.**
(8 marks) (Adapted from BOS, 2010)

There are advantages and disadvantages to gathering data for research from print sources such as books, texts, journals, newspapers and magazines. In general, advantages include a wide availability of the print sources; sustainability of the sources, in that they can be used over and over again; easy reproducibility of the sources; accuracy of some data; and accessibility, since individuals can often access the resources for free in libraries or borrow them from family, friends or colleagues.

The main disadvantages of print sources include storage of the sources and accuracy of some sources, as they may include very general information; print sources are also less easy to access than electronic sources, may be out of date and may have questionable reliability.

Gathering data for research from individuals/groups such as researchers, teachers, experts, businesses people or people directly involved in a study also has its advantages and disadvantages. Advantages include well researched and specialised expert opinions, the ability to clarify issues or questions when accessing the source face to face, ease of access, willingness to participate because of passion/expertise in a certain area and the potential to offer additional leads for the researcher.

Disadvantages of individuals/groups as sources for research include: bias and subjective opinions, validity of data and information provided, possible cost to access these people/individuals, time-consuming data collection, lack of willingness to participate in a study or answer questions, difficulty in fitting into another person's timetable, and the potential for the sample group to not take the research seriously.

Reliability and validity

Students learn about:	Students learn to:
research fundamentals • reliability and validity	• explain how sampling contributes to reliable and valid research

Revision summary

To enhance accuracy in the measurement of data, researchers must adopt the principles of **reliability** and **validity**. **Reliability** is the consistency of measurement. The research is reliable if, were it to be repeated under similar conditions and with the same subjects, the researcher would obtain similar results. **Validity** refers to the accuracy of measurement. The research is valid if it accurately reflects what it was intended to measure.

If researchers conduct background research, use a variety of research methods, choose an appropriate sample group, select a large sample size, and use a combination of sampling methods then the reliability and validity of research will increase as there is less bias and fewer personal judgements made.

Sample examination questions: Multiple choice

6 **A research study is to be conducted into the time spent by students on social media.**
   Which of the following actions would contribute to the validity of the research?
(A) The participants have to be identified.
(B) A case study is conducted in a single school.
(C) Qualitative data is graphed based on the findings.
(D) The student participants are to be randomly selected.
(BOS, 2013)

7 **What would be an indicator of the reliability of a research project?**
(A) The individuals involved are unbiased.
(B) The research method if duplicated will lead to similar results.
(C) The research method has been tested to assess and eliminate problems.
(D) The measurement process accurately reflects what it is intended to measure.
(BOS, 2011)

Sample examination questions: Short answer

6 **Outline the importance of sampling for reliable research.** (3 marks)

Sampling is essential for the collection and presentation of reliable research. The methods used in sampling (from random to stratified), the sample group and the sample size all significantly lead to reliable research.

Reliable research can be obtained by using sampling methods that are specific to the research conducted. For example, using random sampling for sensitive topics is essential for reliable research; otherwise participants may not openly discuss their opinion or feelings. The group chosen as the sample needs to display characteristics and be reflective of the population being researched, enabling accurate and reliable research.

The sample size needs to be of significant value (usually the larger the better) to reflect the number of people being represented in the research. Again, this effectively adds to the importance of sampling for reliable research.

Ethical behaviour

Students learn about:	Students learn to:

research fundamentals
 • ethical behaviour
  – respect
  – integrity
  – privacy
  – bias
	• assess the importance of ethical behaviour when conducting research by considering the following:
	  – sensitive research topics
	  – confidentiality
	  – research bias
	  – crediting sources of data

Revision summary

Ethical behaviour needs to be observed by the researcher when conducting research. Ethical behaviours include BIRP – bias, integrity, respect and privacy.

Bias in research involves the researcher using their personal influence or opinion to affect the data collected. This may include using individuals or groups that they personally know as their subjects (convenience sampling), asking leading questions in questionnaires or interviews, favouring a preconceived position on a topic, avoiding certain questions, altering the answers or observations made in primary research and using samples that do not reflect the intended sample population.

Integrity refers to the honesty and display of strong moral principles shown by the researcher. It can be used to describe behaviour towards the subjects being used in the research, or it can refer to the quality of the data/resources being used to support the findings. Researchers should avoid any sort of bias in their research and be upfront and honest with subjects. They should present the findings that were uncovered, maintain reliability and validity, use reliable research methods, adhere to the rules and guidelines stipulated, display professional conduct, and document data accurately and truthfully. Integrity of data must also be displayed through correct referencing of sources and acknowledgement of individuals and groups, as well as accurate recordkeeping.

Respect can be used alongside integrity, as the subjects being used in the research must be respected and valued. Their opinions, thoughts, feelings, culture, religion, age, gender and health must be respected. Researchers must seek permission firstly to conduct research with the subjects, but also to present any data obtained from the subjects. Informed consent must be gained and permission from parents for underage children must be sought. Researchers should be aware of the development of their questions and approach when conducting research. Subjects should also have the right to refuse to participate or answer a question that could possibly be too personal or sensitive in nature. They have the right to skip questions, have their results destroyed and to see the final product before publication. Researchers must not put any subject in harm's way or at risk.

Privacy needs to be considered through anonymity and confidentiality. Subjects need to be protected and remain anonymous throughout the research process. Names should be changed or coded when referring to subjects. Confidentiality needs to be exhibited through seeking permission of subjects of research, especially when using smartphones and video recording devices. Researchers also need to keep results to themselves, store data carefully during the research and wholly destroy results once they have been used.

Each of these considerations in ethical behaviour is for the protection of the researcher, the subjects and the data collected. They are important in relation to sensitive research topics, maintaining confidentiality, avoiding research bias and crediting sources of data.

Sample examination questions: Multiple choice

8   **Which of the following is an ethical consideration when conducting research?**
(A) Identifying and using all available resources
(B) Examining the limitations of the data collected
(C) Remaining objective throughout the research process
(D) Ensuring that the research methods measure what they are supposed to measure
(BOS, 2013)

9   **Which of the following could lead to bias in an interview?**
(A) The interviewee might give brief responses.
(B) The interviewee might have little knowledge on the topic.
(C) The interviewer might have limited understanding of the topic.
(D) The interviewer might have a pre-existing opinion on the topic.
(BOS, 2012)

10   **How can integrity be maintained in research?**
(A) Use primary data
(B) Check data for validity
(C) Use secondary data to determine results
(D) Collect data that is personal and detailed
(Adapted from BOS, 2012)

11   **Which of the following is an ethical matter that should be considered when conducting research?**
(A) Bias
(B) Privacy
(C) Reliability
(D) Validity
(BOS, 2010)

Sample examination questions: Short answer

7   Outline the strategies a researcher may use:
(a) to protect the privacy of the participants in a study. (3 marks) (BOS, 2013)
To protect the privacy of the participants in a study and to ensure ethical behaviour, a researcher could adopt a number of strategies including: considering the sensitive nature of some research topics; asking participant permission to record research responses and findings; ensuring all results remain confidential by changing the name or any identifying object on results published; employing secure storage of results; disposing of private information carefully; and maintaining anonymity of participants to other participants and the researcher.

(b) to show respect for subjects of research. (3 marks) (BOS, 2013)
To show respect for subjects of research in order to ensure ethical behaviour, a researcher could also adopt further strategies in addition to those used to protect privacy. These may include: seeking the consent and willingness of participants to be part of the research; analysing the body language of participants and ceasing the conduct of research if they start to become uncomfortable; caring for the social, physical, emotional and spiritual needs of the participants; respecting their religious, cultural and physical differences; offering thanks and appreciation for their participation; and reminding them that they can cease participating at any time or have their results destroyed before being used.

8   Evaluate the significance of bias and sampling when conducting research. (6 marks) (BOS, 2011)

It is profoundly significant to avoid bias and to apply sampling appropriately when conducting research. Bias is the unfair application of a number of factors that could change or influence the results of research. Bias may include the researcher's personal beliefs, feelings, opinions, judgement, relationship and subjectivity to the issues and/or participants in the research process. All of these could impact negatively on the collection, analysis and conclusion of research, leading to inaccurate results. In addition, bias can adversely affect the findings and results of research, therefore reducing reliability and validity of the data collected.

Sampling can be used in an influential manner when conducting research. Sampling is the choice of people, places and times to collect research data. By using a variety of appropriate research methods, a suitable sample group and a large sample size, a researcher can ensure that their results are valid and reliable. On the other hand, if a researcher becomes complacent in their approach and uses limited sampling methods, an inappropriate sample group or a small sample size, research can be impacted negatively.

Consequently, if appropriate sampling is not achieved, the research data can be biased and therefore valid conclusions cannot be made from the research collected.

9   **Assess the importance of ethical behaviour in relation to sensitive natures of research topics.** (5 marks)

Respect in relation to research is crucial as it ensures that bias does not occur with the sensitive nature of the topic being researched, such as a one-sided view of teen pregnancy. Respect is crucial in order for the researcher to gain trust so that the data collected is honest, truthful (to ensure the results are reliable) and valid.

Integrity relates to the morality of the research and the truthfulness and honesty of the data collected. When researching, if the topic is sensitive to the individual's own previous experiences, it may bring up traumatic and emotional reactions. Questions must be asked in a respectful manner, which will support the interviewee so their responses will be honest and truthful. This will ensure that the data is reliable and valid.

Privacy refers to the non-disclosure of personal or identifiable characteristics of the subject. This is very important when researching sensitive research topics. If the subject thinks there is a risk that their responses could be made public they may not be open to giving data or their data may not be honest or truthful, which will limit the reliability and validity of the study.

Bias refers to the research being manipulated either intentionally or unintentionally to suit the hypothesis or research question. For example, the researcher may change the results of answers given or offer questions that lead the subject in a particular direction. When researching sensitive research topics, it is important to offer unbiased questions because manipulated questions may cause further trauma or anxiety to the subject.

Research methods

Students learn about:	Students learn to:
research methods • questionnaires • interviews • case studies • observations • literature reviews	• describe each research methodology and evaluate the suitability of each for different research topics • select and utilise appropriate research methods to conduct research

Revision summary

Researchers can select from a variety of different *research methods*, such as questionnaires, interviews, case studies, observations and literature reviews, to use in their research. A combination of the research methods can improve the reliability and validity of the data obtained.

Questionnaires can obtain both quantitative and qualitative data through the use of open and closed questions. The presentation of the questionnaire is made easy through the use of many online tools, or traditional forms can still be used. Distribution and collection can be done in person, over the phone, via email or other electronic means. Data collection and interpretation can be relatively straightforward as questions are generally easy to answer and do not require many detailed responses, especially closed questions.

Interviews are another form of survey where questions are asked of individuals or groups face to face, on the phone or via any other technology such as video conferencing, smartphones, webcam or email. Interviews can be formally structured, where there are set questions developed beforehand, or unstructured, which is more casual in nature and questions are developed in a conversational manner. Recording and interpreting data is more difficult for interviews because of the nature of questions and the responses. This can be done via pen and paper, but with permission any form of technology, such as Dictaphone, smartphone, camcorder or iPad, would make it much easier.

Observations are made of individuals or groups in a certain environment and how they behave or respond is recorded. Researchers can engage in participant observation, where the researcher observes from within, or non-participant observation, where the subject/s are not interacting with the researcher. Data can be recorded through notes or images by the researcher while the session is taking place or, with permission, the session can be recorded to view later. Data analysis can be done through the detailed notes made, recordings watched and diagrams/graphs created. Observations may be subject to bias possibly due to interaction with the researcher, knowledge of observation, change in subject behaviour or the accuracy of recording.

Case studies are detailed investigations conducted over time (possibly even weeks, months or years) on a particular focus area, issue, individual, group or organisation. Case studies are developed using a number of primary research methods as well as secondary data that already exists. Researchers may choose to use pre-existing secondary case studies. Case studies can be difficult to develop as they are intended to show a process or how a change has occurred. They can be subjective, and researchers may find it difficult not to become involved and thus influence the results.

Literature reviews can be developed by researchers in response to the review of different pre-existing secondary sources that relate to the focus of the research. Literature reviews provide background and supportive material to the focus of research. Sources that can be used to create a literature review include books, journals, online sources, newspapers, article or other relevant secondary sources. All sources must be cited correctly within the literature review and then acknowledged correctly in the bibliography.

Each research method has both advantages and limitations and is suitable for a variety of different research topics.

Sample examination questions: Multiple choice

12 Jordan is conducting research into the community's view on the legislation of same sex marriage.
    Which type of research would give the widest selection of viewpoints?
(A) Case study
(B) Interview
(C) Observation
(D) Questionnaire
(BOSTES, 2014)

13 **What is the main advantage of using a questionnaire when conducting research?**
(A) It can provide a large amount of data quickly.
(B) It can provide in-depth data over a period of time.
(C) It can enable the researcher to watch and record behaviours.
(D) It enables existing data to be used to gain background information.
(BOS, 2013)

14 **A researcher wants to conduct a detailed investigation of the use of technology by families over time.**
    Which research methodology would be best suited to this purpose?
(A) Interview
(B) Case study
(C) Observation
(D) Questionnaire
(BOS, 2013)

15 **Which research methodology is the most suitable to gain information about the leisure activities of high school students in Australia?**
(A) Observation
(B) Questionnaire
(C) Structured interview
(D) Unstructured interview
(BOS, 2011)

16   Which of the following best describes a literature review?
(A) A qualitative investigation of a particular issue
(B) A summary of information on a particular topic
(C) An analysis of primary information on a particular topic
(D) A detailed study of both primary and secondary information
(BOS, 2011)

17   What information should a literature review provide?
(A) An analysis of the data collected
(B) A hypothesis with focus questions
(C) A summary of information already written about the topic
(D) An outline of limitations associated with the research procedures used
(BOS, 2010)

Sample examination questions: Short answer

10   Why are interview and questionnaires appropriate methods of research to test the hypothesis, 'The aged today are technologically skilled'?
(4 marks) (BOSTES, 2014)

Interviews and questionnaires are highly appropriate methods of research to test the above hypothesis as the researcher gains first-hand information through primary research.

Interviews involve asking a series of structured or unstructured questions to seek people's opinions, viewpoint or feelings about an issue. It is possible that an unstructured approach may make the aged individuals more comfortable when responding. Using various electronic means, such as video cameras, Dictaphones, smartphones and tablets, to record responses of the aged could also assist in proving or disproving the hypothesis by their openness or reservation in using the technology. Using interviews with aged individuals would be highly appropriate as they can clarify questions while they are being asked, whether it is face to face or on the phone, and they may enjoy the personal contact and feel valued through their participation. The researcher can also judge whether the aged individuals understand the questions asked and provide them with further support around the questions.

Questionnaires are also an appropriate method of research as they allow for a large amount of data to be collected in a straightforward manner. Questionnaires are a series of prepared open or closed questions and can be quick to use and easy to distribute. This would prove beneficial for aged individuals, as questionnaires are not too time consuming to complete if the participants receive support in writing their responses. Aged individuals may feel comfortable to respond to certain questions privatively, anonymously and at a time that suits them.

11 Compare a case study and an observation as methods of collecting data when conducting research. (4 marks) (BOS, 2011)

Case studies and observations as methods of collecting data when conducting research have some similarities and differences. Case studies are detailed studies conducted over time and observations are recordings about the behaviour of a subject.

Both of these methods of research are time consuming, require background information about the subjects being researched, can be quite subjective, collect in-depth information and are used in conjunction with other primary research methods.

The differences between the two methods include the method of recording, presentation of results, and inclination towards bias observations due to researcher involvement. Case studies tend to be more reliable as they use a variety of primary research methods and there could be more crucial information observed or discussed during observations.

Research process

Students learn about:	Students learn to:
research process	

• planning for research
  – formulating a research proposal
  – managing resources, e.g. time, materials
• conducting research
  – accessing sources of data
  – collecting and recording data
  – documenting actions and issues
• interpreting research
  – presenting research findings
  – analysing research results
  – drawing conclusions from research
	• apply the research process to a chosen topic by:
	  – selecting a research focus
	  – selecting appropriate sampling methods
	  – proposing how the research will be conducted
	  – creating a timeline for research goals
	  – accessing relevant sources of secondary data
	  – using suitable research methods to collect and record primary and secondary data
	  – recording actions and proposing solutions to any research issues
	  – presenting primary data in graphs, tables or written reports
	  – comparing key findings from primary and secondary data
	  – forming research-based conclusions and making recommendations
	  – crediting sources of data by means of bibliography and appendix

Revision summary

The *research process* is a lengthy one that can span over months, years or even decades. The research process presented in the CAFS syllabus is a 12-step process, with the twelfth step being the submission of the report.

The research process follows three main stages – **planning for research**, **conducting research** and **interpreting research**.

Planning for research includes formulating a research proposal in which researchers develop a project plan, which is an initial summary and outline of the research process. This stage would include selecting a research focus, selecting appropriate sampling methods, proposing how the research will be conducted and creating a timeline for research goals. It also involves the researcher managing their resources such as time through planning and materials such as a tablet/laptop, recording devices, note pads and folders needed to conduct the research.

After the planning stage, a researcher will start **conducting research**. This involves accessing sources of data through individuals, groups, print and digital sources. Included in this would be accessing relevant sources of secondary data and using suitable research methods to collect and record primary and secondary data. The next step would involve <u>collecting and recording data</u>. This could be through a variety of research methods and using a number of different recording devices. While conducting research, researchers would be <u>documenting actions and issues</u> through recording actions and proposing solutions to any research issues.

The researcher may create a record of the ongoing process through a diary, which may be presented in hand-written form, in folders, electronically, via a mind-map, using a video, in a journal, via a blog or some other form of recording. This diary should reflect the proposed timeline and would record the values, attitudes and feelings of the researcher. It should reflect honestly on problems encountered and their solutions. The diary could be used to record readings, conversations, contacts and sources of secondary data.

The last stage of the research process involves **interpreting research**. This is done through <u>presenting research findings </u>by using both quantitative data in graphs, tables and statistics as well as qualitative data through detailed descriptions of the data discovered. <u>Analysing research results</u> would involve comparing key findings from primary and secondary data to develop a comprehensive analysis of the results discovered. Finally, <u>drawing conclusions from research</u> would involve the researcher forming research-based conclusions, discussing the overall findings of the investigation, linking this to the hypothesis or focus question, what was learnt, how valid and reliable the findings were, and making recommendations as to what might be done differently next time. The researcher would ensure that they are crediting sources of data by the means of a correctly formatted bibliography (and throughout the project). The researcher can also develop a clearly numbered and labelled appendix should they wish to include any supporting materials that did not fit in the main body of the report, such as interview questions, any copies of raw data, key secondary articles used or interview transcripts.

The project is then ready for presentation, submission and review.

Sample examination questions: Multiple choice

18 Which of the following should be placed in the appendix of a research project?
(A) A copy of any chapter referred to in the project
(B) Copies of the journals from which articles were used
(C) A written copy of any research questions and responses
(D) The bibliography with all relevant sources of information
(BOSTES, 2014)

19 Which of the following is a requirement when undertaking a research project?
(A) Using visual representation of data
(B) Working collaboratively
(C) Conducting a pilot study
(D) Acknowledging copyright and sources
(BOSTES, 2014)

20 When conducting research, what is the next step after the research proposal has been formulated?
(A) Collecting and recording data
(B) Analysing and interpreting data
(C) Presenting data in tables and graphs
(D) Selecting appropriate research methods
(BOS, 2013)

Use the following information to answer Questions 21–24.

A research study was conducted from 2008–2011 on a large number of young people living in Australia. Young people aged 11 to 24 years were asked to indicate their top three issues of personal concern from the list. The table shows the issues of greatest concern and the percentages of young people who identified these as concerns.

Issues of personal concern to young people

Concerns	2008 (%)	2009 (%)	2010 (%)	2010 (%)
School or study problems	18.6	17.3	25.5	37.3
Coping with stress	20.4	18.7	27.3	35.4
Body image	26.3	25.5	31.1	33.1
Family conflict	25.9	24.1	27.8	28.1
Drugs	26.0	26.8	20.5	16.9

21 Which type of research methodology was most likely used to obtain the data in the table?
(A) Case study
(B) Observation
(C) Questionnaire
(D) Structured interview
(BOS, 2012)

22 The results of the research study are to be represented on ONE graph. Which type of graph would most likely clearly represent these results?
(A) Cluster
(B) Column
(C) Line
(D) Pie (sector)
(BOS, 2012)

23 What trend do these findings best reflect about young people's issues of personal concern?
(A) Personal concern about drugs has steadily decreased.
(B) Body image has consistently been a personal concern.
(C) Family conflict has decreased as a matter of personal concern.
(D) Personal concern about school or study problems will continue to increase.
(BOS, 2012)

24 The results of this study have proven to be reliable.
Which of the following factors would have contributed to reliability?
(A) The research questions were modified over time.
(B) The research questions were all of similar length.
(C) The study was conducted in the capital cities of Australia.
(D) The study was conducted in the same range of communities across
     Australia.
(BOS, 2012)

Use the graph shown to answer Questions 25 and 26.

The graph shows the percentage of school-aged children who play a team sport.

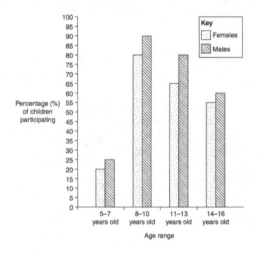

25 Which age range has the largest percentage difference between male
    and female?
(A) 5–7 years old
(B) 8–10 years old
(C) 11–13 years old
(D) 14–16 years old
(BOS, 2011)

26 Which statement is supported by the data in the graph?
(A) Males and females of all ages are very active.
(B) Females don't enjoy playing a team sport as much as males.
(C) A greater percentage of males than females play a team sport.
(D) More males from the 5–10 age ranges play in a team sport than those in the
     11–16 age ranges.
(BOS, 2011)

Use the following table to answer Questions 27 and 28.

In 2002, a survey was conducted of people aged 65 to 74 attending cultural venues and events. The table shows the survey data about the venue and events attended.

Venue or event attended	Age group Males 65–74 Females 65–74
Art galleries	19.3 25.2
Museums	19.0 21.7
Zoological parks and aquariums	24.1 25.5
Botanic gardens	40.3 39.4
Libraries	36.8 37.8
Classical musical concerts	9.2 12.8
Popular music concerts	12.1 11.8
Theatre performances	11.4 18.3
Dance performance	6.4 11.3
Musicals and operas	14.2 24.0
Other performing arts	14.3 14.7
Cinemas	41.5 46.8
At least one venue or event	73.1 78.9

27 Which of the following statements is best supported by data in this table?
(A) Art gallerias are the most attended cultural venues.
(B) Men are more likely than women to attend cultural events.
(C) Women are more likely than men to attend popular music concerts.
(D) Most people aged 65–74 who were surveyed attend cultural events.
(BOS, 2010)

28 What was the most likely method of data collection for this survey?
(A) Case study
(B) Interview
(C) Observation
(D) Random sample
(BOS, 2010)

29 What information is most likely to be provided on a graph?
(A) Qualitative information
(B) Date in table format
(C) A numerical representation of data
(D) Data obtained from primary research
(BOS, 2010)

30 Which of the following is an item that may be included in an appendix of a research report?
(A) A summary of secondary research
(B) Interview questions used for the research
(C) A list of presentation methods used to produce the report
(D) Acknowledgement of using someone else's work in the research
(BOS, 2010)

Sample examination questions: Short answer

12 Describe what should be included in a written report on a research project. (7 marks) (BOSTES, 2014)

There are various aspects to be included in a written report on a research project. These include a title, contents, introduction, literature review, results, analysis, discussion and conclusion, bibliography and appendix.

A suitable title and accurate contents page provide a good structure for the research project and precede the actual written report.

The first item to appear in a written report is an introduction. It provides the reader with an overview of what the research project is about, what the focus question or hypothesis is, and what research methodologies were used, and it acknowledges individuals and groups that supported or were part of the research project.

This is then followed by a literature review, which provides to the reader background or already existing information that has been obtained from secondary sources such as books, journal articles and research papers. It is used to support the findings that are gathered through primary research.

Following this are the results, which can be presented quantitatively or qualitatively. This can be done through graphs, tables and statistics obtained from the primary data that was collated. Raw data is tabulated and converted into percentages and presented in the form of a graph so trends and comparisons can be made.

The results are then compared to the secondary research and presented in the analysis. Here researchers will present their careful analysis of primary and secondary data. This means that researchers need to look for trends, patterns, observations and relationships between all sets of quantitative and qualitative data.

The key findings of the research project are presented in the discussion and conclusion. This depicts the researcher's overall findings and relates specifically to the focus question and whether or not it was answered, or whether or not the hypothesis was supported or refuted. Researchers can also make mention to the reliability and validity of the findings as well as possible implications and recommendations from the research.

An accurate bibliography in alphabetical order provides an acknowledgement of all sources used throughout the research project. It can be structured using a variety of styles such as American Psychological Association (APA), Oxford or Harvard. The appendix, if it is included, completes the written report and includes any data or information that could not fit into the main body of the project such as key journal articles, raw data, photographs, transcripts of interview, and blank questionnaires. These need to be labelled accordingly with a title and a number.

13   What are the features of a bibliography and an appendix? (4 marks)
(BOS, 2012)

Features of a bibliography and an appendix are used as supporting documents to a research project; both are included at the end of a written report and follow a specific structure.

Bibliographies are used to cite all of the primary and secondary sources used in the research project. Features include the accuracy of a bibliography through various styles such as APA, Oxford or Harvard. The chosen style needs to be maintained throughout the bibliography. The sources are listed in alphabetical order via the author's last name, and include a year of publication, a title, type and place of publication and publisher.

An appendix entails any documents or supporting evidence that could not fit or may not be appropriate to include in a written report. Features may also include a title and number for each item, key journal articles, blank questionnaires, interview transcripts, raw data, photographs or significant newspaper articles.

Chapter 2

Groups in Context

This module should occupy approximately 25 per cent of total course time.
This module builds upon students' knowledge and understanding acquired in the Preliminary course modules Resource Management and Individuals and Groups.

Students explore FOUR specific groups within the community who may be experiencing inequities by examining the nature of the group, their specific needs and level of access to services.

Students undertake a detailed investigation of TWO groups to examine the role that positive social environments can have on enhancing the wellbeing of the group and individuals within the group.
(BOS, 2013, p. 29).

HSC core 2: Groups in Context

Mandatory category A: People with disabilities

<table>
<tr>
<td colspan="2" align="center">Category A groups
(Mandatory groups)
• People with disabilities
• Homeless people</td>
</tr>
<tr>
<td>Students learn about:</td>
<td>Students learn to:</td>
</tr>
<tr>
<td>exploring the four specific groups within the community
• prevalence of each group within the community
• individual diversity within each group
• terminology used by the community to describe the group</td>
<td>• utilise reliable sources of data to examine the nature of each group by considering the following questions:
  – what is the prevalence of the group within Australia?
  – what determines whether an individual is part of the group?
  – how might individuals vary within the group?
• recognise that the community uses positive and negative terminology to describe each group. Discuss the impact this might have on individuals within the group</td>
</tr>
</table>

Revision summary

When **exploring** people with disabilities **within the community** it is essential to look at the **prevalence of the group within the community, individual diversity within each group** and **terminology used by the community to describe the group.** This can be remembered by the acronym PIT.

There are varying definitions used to _determine whether an individual is part of this group_. The World Health Organization (2016) uses disabilities as an umbrella term that includes impairments, activity limitations and participation restrictions. The United Nations Convention on the Rights of Persons with Disabilities (United Nations, 2006) defines those who have long-term physical, mental, intellectual or sensory impairments which, in interaction with various barriers, may hinder their full and effective participation in society on an equal basis with others.

The **prevalence of this group within the community**, specifically _within Australia,_ is represented by 18.5% of the population or approximately 4.2 million people. Six per cent or 1.4 million people have a profound disability. The prevalence of disability in Australia fell by 1.5 percentage points between 2003 and 2012, with a correlation between age and disability throughout the whole time period. A smaller proportion of males with disability than females were prevalent (18% compared with 19%) (Australian Bureau of Statistics, 2012).

Individual diversity within the group and _how individuals might vary within the group_ People with disabilities is best represented by the acronym PIPS. People with disabilities can have an impairment that is physical such as a cerebral palsy or spina bifida, intellectual such as developmental delays or Down syndrome, psychological such as schizophrenia or depression, or sensory such as visual/hearing impairment or autism.

Various **terminology is used by the community to describe the group** People with disabilities. This includes both _positive and negative terminology to describe_ the group, which has an _impact on individuals within the group_. _Positive terminology_ used by the community to _describe the group_ is reflected by a change in attitude, understanding and recognition that a person should not be defined by their disability. An example of positive terminology is having a 'lucky fin' (from the movie _Finding Nemo_), which are the terms used to describe individuals with upper limb differences. _Negative terminology_ that is derogatory, judgemental, patronising and/or offensive such as 'special', 'invalid', 'the deaf', 'retard', 'spastic' or 'psycho' should be replaced by positive and accepted terms such as 'person with a disability', 'person with Down syndrome' or 'person with a mental illness'. The change from negative to positive terminology will _impact_ a person with a disability by making them feel safe, accepted and respected instead of judged, discriminated and disrespected.

Sample examination questions: Short answer

1   **For people with disabilities outline the impact positive and negative terminology might have on the individuals within the group.** (4 marks)

By using the term 'people with disabilities' we are recognising the importance of identifying individuals as people, not by their disability. Other appropriate terms may be specific to the disability such as 'a person with a physical disability' or 'a person with a mental illness'. The impact of using this sort of positive terminology is meaningful as people will feel supported, accepted and a sense of self-worth.

On the other hand, derogatory and negative terminology can be extremely detrimental to the wellbeing of people with a disability. Using words such as a 'disabled person', 'amputee', 'cripple', 'the blind' and 'special' fails to recognise the individual. It can degrade and diminish an individual's self-esteem and confidence to socialise, as well as make them feel unsafe and unwelcome. An individual's disability need not be mentioned at all, unless it is necessary in the context of the situation or discussion.

NB: You can insert the Homeless or any of the category B groups studied and answer the same questions accordingly.

Issues of concern

Students learn about:	Students learn to:

issues of concern for the four specific groups within the community
satisfaction of needs
• specific needs of each group
   – adequate standard of living (food, clothing, shelter)
   – health
   – education
   – employment
   – safety and security
   – sense of identity
access to services
• types of services, e.g. financial support, transport, accommodation and housing, health care, counselling, education, employment, legal aid
• factors affecting access to services
   – characteristics of individuals within the group, e.g. age, gender, level of education, culture, type of disability, first language spoken, socioeconomic status
   – resources, e.g. time, money, energy, knowledge
   – aspects of the service, e.g. opening hours, confidentiality, location, staffing
	• identify and prioritise the specific needs of each group
	
	• justify the TWO most significant needs for each group and discuss the implications if these are not met
	
	• explore the factors that can affect each group's access to services by considering the following questions:
	   – what types of services does each group require access to?
	   – how do the characteristics of individuals within each group affect their access to services?
	   – what resources are necessary to support each group's access to the service?
	   – how available are the services within the community?

Revision summary

There are **issues of concern for** people with disabilities including *satisfaction of needs* and *access to services*.

The *satisfaction of needs* is an issue of concern and includes specific needs of each group such as HESEAS – adequate standard of living (food, clothing, shelter), health, education, employment, safety and security, and sense of identity. These specific needs to have to be *prioritised* and *justified* and all of them have *implications if these are not met*.

Health is paramount to the wellbeing of people with disabilities. Knowledge of the health issues specifically related to the disability needs to be developed. Medicare, government incentives and private health insurance will need to be used to pay for the medications, treatment, equipment and care that might be required such as physiotherapy, pharmaceuticals, wheelchairs, hearing aids, glasses and prosthetics. Family members, friends or carers may need to be relied on for the management of health issues such as daily tasks, lifting and medication administration. The combination of these issues may also impact negatively on the emotional factors affecting the wellbeing of people with disabilities.

Education is another priority for people with disabilities. Specialised care and treatment needs to be explored and investigated to manage the disability. Carers also need to receive adequate education and training to support the dependant they are caring for. Education at school age needs to be considered, with mainstream schooling being a preferred option. Possible modifications to equipment may be needed, such as lowered desks, modifications to tasks and support from a diversity/special education team. Further education and training will also need to be considered so people with a disability have the same post-school opportunities.

People with a disability may have low self-esteem and their sense of identity may be strained due to the frustration, sadness and potential embarrassment they might feel because of their disability. Alternatively, other people with a disability may feel a positive sense of identity and it may not affect them at all. If they are working in education, training or some sort if advocacy role, their sense of identity may be heightened.

The need for employment will depend on the extent of the disability and the support people with disabilities receive. Some people with disabilities may be able to maintain a stable job, others may find it difficult due to the treatment, care, physical/cognitive tasks or possibly the attitude of the employers. Ongoing education and training is important as well as possible modifications to job tasks. Community organisations such as Disability Works or the House with No Steps have developed programs to assist people with disabilities in the workforce. Employment would help to satisfy many needs of a person with a disability as well as help them to feel a sense of contribution and accomplishment.

People with disabilities need an adequate standard of living, but this may be difficult to access due to their lack of finances because of their possible inability to have full-time employment. Carers and community organisations such as Meals on Wheels and St Vincent de Paul have important roles to play in the accessibility of basic needs for people with disabilities. Grocery shopping, preparation of nutritious meals, appropriate clothing choices, alterations to clothing, modification of the physical environment and maintenance of the home are tasks that might need to be undertaken either with or without the support of people with disabilities.

Safety and security is important. Modification of the physical environment may be needed, such as installation of ramps, rails, or low temperature taps. Emotional needs must be recognised by providing support through counselling or personal development programs. Social needs must be catered for by providing opportunities to gather with other people, such as in outings to the movies or discussion and support in mutual self-help groups. Financial needs are also important through the provision of government support such as the Disability Support Pension, parking permits, subsidies through Medicare and the PBS. Community organisations can also help with such things as affordable second-hand clothing or equipment. People with disabilities might also consider installing security cameras, gates or back-to-base alarms because they are often the target of robberies, assaults or abuse in some instances.

Access to services is also an issue of concern for people with disabilities and includes **types of services** and **factors affecting access to services**.

Types of services include aspects such as financial support, transport, accommodation and housing, health care, counselling, education, employment and legal aid.

Financial support can be provided through a variety of different programs, schemes, subsidies, allowances, reimbursements and government incentives such as Mobility Allowance and Child Disability Allowance. Community groups such as charitable (Assistance Dogs Australia), religious (Wesley Disability Services) or private (People with Disability) organisations may provide goods, services and support to people with disabilities.

Disability Standards for Accessible Public Transport (2002) has driven improvements and equitable access for transport services. Such services provided by the government and other organisations on public transport may include the low-floor design buses offered on many routes throughout Australia, platform to train boarding ramps, ramped access on Sydney ferries, colour-contrasting handrails and signage, provision of guide dogs/service animals, lifts and wheelchair spaces. Disabled car parking permits for drivers/carers, designated parking spaces for people with mobility disabilities, wheelchair accessible taxis and free community transport from shops or leisure centres are other examples of transport services.

Accommodation and housing services include permanent, temporary and crisis or modifications required for a person with a disability to stay safely. These may include public housing, rental housing, purpose-built rental, home modifications, supported accommodation and community housing. Applications, assessments and interviews are conducted alongside many of these arrangements.

The services provided by health care are of great significance to the treatment and enhancement of wellbeing for people with disabilities. Health care services may include those provided by hospitals, medical centres, doctors, surgeons, nurses, general practitioners, pharmacies, specialists, physiotherapists, optometrists and occupational therapists. Medicare, private health insurance, out-of-pocket expenses and government schemes are all considerations with these health care services.

The impact of factors influencing the emotional wellbeing of a person with a disability may mean that they may need to access counselling on a permanent or temporary basis. These services can be provided through the government, in workplaces, hospitals or medical centres and are conducted by psychologists, counsellors, doctors, nurses, carers and social workers.

Education services provide people with disabilities with a range of support through gaining knowledge about the nature, treatment and management of a disability. Examples include specialised services, childcare, mainstream schools, colleges, VET and TAFE, private organisations, government programs, community colleges, tutorials, online learning and home programs.

Services provided through employment aim to support people with disabilities in learning new skills, mastering pre-existing skills, learning on the job, providing apprenticeships, gaining experience and completing training. Support is provided for both the employer and employee to maximise the experience of success for people with disabilities in the workforce. Examples may include Nova Employment, Ability Options and Disability Employment Services.

Legal aid provides people with disabilities with free or discounted legal assistance through the government or organisations such as Australian Centre for Disability Law and Intellectual Disability Rights Service on matters pertaining to discrimination, treatment, advocacy, law and policies.

Factors affecting access to services can be remembered by the acronym CAR. Characteristics of individuals within the group; e.g. first language spoken, culture, socioeconomic status, type of disability, age, gender, level of education (Lights. Camera. STAGE); aspects of the service, e.g. location, opening hours, confidentiality, staffing (LOCS); and resources, e.g. knowledge, energy, money, time (KEMT).

Characteristics of individuals within the group People with Disabilities affect their access to services. The first language spoken may be different to the information available to people with disabilities; fear or embarrassment may then prevent them from gaining access. Interpreters or translators may need to be used for individuals to access the service. Culture may also affect their access due to restrictions, beliefs or language barriers. Socioeconomic status may affect access to specialised services such as rehabilitation, occupational therapy or involvement in leisure pursuits due the high costs involved in treatment, care and equipment. The type of disability may improve, limit or inhibit access to certain services as most specialise in a specific type of disability. The gender of a person with a disability would unlikely impact their access to services, but the gender of the employees working for the service might create some potential embarrassment issues. The level of education of a person with a disability might affect their knowledge of the functions of services available. This might also correlate with socioeconomic status.

Aspects of the service such as location might impact on the ease of access for people with disabilities. If they are living in a rural or remote community and specialised services are based in the city, they may need to rely on public transport (and possibly overnight accommodation) with the hope that it has been modified to accommodate people with disabilities. The physical location of services also needs to be easily accessible to people with disabilities by offering ramps, lifts, handrails and plenty of disabled parking. Opening hours of services need to be considered in terms of accessibility with a working carer/family member/friend and the individual managing their everyday tasks. Offering out of regular hours support may be of benefit to many carers, as would access to 24-hour online support. Confidentiality needs to remain a priority and should be paramount to the operations of the service in order to respect all individuals. In addition, laws and policies such as the *Disability Discrimination Act 1992* protect people with disabilities from having to disclose their disability. Staffing needs to be constantly monitored within services for the ease and access of people with disabilities. These individuals should receive ongoing education and training on how to best support and respect people with disabilities.

Resources such as knowledge will either hinder or help people with disabilities in their access of services. Self-expression or communication issues might impact on the ability of a person with a disability to gain knowledge of services. If an individual does not know about the services or features of services available to them they might not be able to manage their disability effectively. People with disabilities may have a number of health issues that may impact on their energy levels and therefore their motivation and willingness to access services. Money availability, or lack of it, may put stress on a person with a disability due to the high costs associated with treatment, care and specialised equipment such as wheelchairs or even glasses. People with disabilities often have limited time available, possibly due to how long it takes to do everyday tasks in addition to attending a number of specialists appointments, using public transport or waiting for carers/family or friends to help them access services.

Sample examination questions: Multiple choice

1   Which of the following would be most beneficial for the social wellbeing of an elderly disabled person living in a retirement village?
(A) Access to hospitals
(B) Private health insurance
(C) Leisure facilities and community transport
(D) Temporary accommodation and counselling services
(Adapted from BOSTES, 2014)

**2   Billy is a person with a disability who lives with his elderly mother and is completing his HSC.
Which of the following are the most significant needs for Billy?**
(A) Adequate standard of living and sense of identity
(B) Health and security and safety
(C) Employment and education
(D) Adequate standard of living and employment
(Adapted from BOS, 2012)

3   Which of the following factors are most likely to affect access for a blind person who has obtained employment in the city?
(A) Legislation and technology
(B) Employment history and age of children
(C) Availability of transport and location of housing
(D) Types of available services and number of children
(BOS, 2013)

4   Which of a person's needs may be the most affected when they have a disability that limits their ability to perform household and family roles?
(A) Education
(B) Employment
(C) Safety and security
(D) Sense of identity
(BOS, 2011)

5   **Which of the following would have safety and security as their most significant needs?**
(A) A person with a disability who has recently become unemployed
(B) A person with a vision impairment who is living alone
(C) An elderly couple living on the streets
(D) A person who is living in a refuge
(Adapted from BOS, 2011)

Sample examination questions: Short answer

2   **Identify types of services that people with disabilities require access to and outline the resources that are necessary to support the group's access to the services.** (5 marks)

The types of services that people with disabilities require access to can be influenced by resources which are necessary to support the group's access to the services.

Types of services such as financial support through Centrelink in the form of Mobility and Child Disability Allowance require knowledge that the service exists. Researching various private organisations that offer support such as Assistance Dogs Australia and Wesley Mission Disability Services requires time and energy to investigate.

Access to transport, accommodation and housing services such as wheelchair accessible taxis, free community transport from shops, crisis accommodation and purpose built rental homes require people with disability to both have knowledge of the services, and the time and energy to explore them.

People with disabilities may need access to specialised care or health services in order to manage their disability. Resources such as time and money may be necessary to support the group's access to the services as there may be lengthy delays in wait times, physical assessment and money to pay for some of these special services.

Education services often provide people with disabilities with a range of support through gaining understanding about the nature, treatment and management of a disability. Individuals may need to be knowledgeable and have the energy to discover community education programs offered to support people with disabilities.

3   **Discuss the implications when the TWO most significant needs of people with disabilities are not met.** (8 marks)

There are significant implications for people with disabilities when their most significant needs of health and safety and security are not met.

Health is essential to the wellbeing and satisfaction of needs for people with disabilities. Due to the specialised care and treatment often associated with some types of disabilities, an individual needs to ensure that they keep health as a high priority. If the health needs of people with disabilities are compromised then other health-related issues might result, needing immediate attention and action and/or possibly creating further health issues down the track, including lowered quality of life and a reduced life span. This could have a further implication on family members and/or carers as it would put more demand on their role in supporting the person with a disability, leading to possible feelings of resentment or inability to cope.

When the health needs of people with disabilities are not met, dangerous implications to their immune system or physical or psychological functioning could result. If people with disabilities fail to attend a medical consultation or procedure or take medications incorrectly it could possibly do further damage to their condition, resulting in deterioration, additional treatment or possibly hospitalisation. The damage done could further heighten feelings of self-doubt and lowered self-esteem or possibly lead to depression. This in turn has an impact on their financial situation as there would be additional costs incurred, which could place further pressure on the socioeconomic status and sense of identity of people with disabilities.

Safety and security is a significant need for people with disabilities to have a safe and adequate standard of living. Due to the vulnerability of people with disabilities and the specialised care required to support their wellbeing, it is essential that people with disabilities are safe and secure. If modifications such as ramps, rails and low temperature taps are not made, then people with disabilities may feel unsafe, which could put them in a state of high alertness and on edge, possibly leading to anxiety. In turn this would affect their self-worth, as they do not feel safe in their own environment. Modifications to the physical environment could also include installing security cameras, gates or back-to-base alarms, especially because people with disabilities may be the target of robberies, assaults or even abuse in some instances. If these strategies to ensure safety and security are not achieved, people with disabilities may feel extremely vulnerable and exposed to danger, which can affect their overall wellbeing.

Financial security could also be impacted if safety and security needs are not met. People with disabilities may need to be supported by their families and carers in the management of their monetary requirements and what they need and want to purchase with any income they earn or financial support they receive from Centrelink or other private organisations. If financial security is not met, people with disabilities may be faced with financial difficulties and budgeting issues, resulting in a lowered sense of self-worth and self-esteem. People with disabilities therefore will become more reliant on government support for an adequate standard of living.

NB: You can insert the Homeless or any of the category B groups studied and answer the same questions accordingly.

Mandatory category A: Homeless people

Category A groups **(Mandatory groups)** • People with disabilities • Homeless people		
Students learn about:	**Students learn to:**	

exploring the four specific groups within the community
• prevalence of each group within the community
• individual diversity within each group
• terminology used by the community to describe the group
	• utilise reliable sources of data to examine the nature of each group by considering the following questions:
	  – what is the prevalence of the group within Australia?
	  – what determines whether an individual is part of the group?
	  – how might individuals vary within the group?
	• recognise that the community uses positive and negative terminology to describe each group. Discuss the impact this might have on individuals within the group.	

Revision summary

When **exploring** the homeless **within the community** it is essential to look at the **prevalence of the group within the community, individual diversity within each group** and **terminology used by the community to describe the group.** This can be remembered by the acronym PIT.

There are many definitions of homelessness, which can all be combined to a simpler notion that the homeless are a group of people who all have inadequate access to safe and secure housing.

The **prevalence of this group within the community**, specifically *within Australia*, is approximately 1 in every 200 people, according to Homelessness Australia (http://www.homelessnessaustralia.org.au). This is approximately 105 237 people who are homeless on any given night.

Individual diversity within the group and *how individuals might vary within the group* implies that the simple notion of the above definition, which groups together all people who have inadequate safe and secure housing, does not take into account the large range of diversity within that group.

Levels of inadequate housing are encompassed by Mackenzie and Chamberlain's (1992) definition (*Homelessness Australia*), which includes three categories in the recognition of the diversity of homelessness:

- Primary homelessness is experienced by people without conventional accommodation (e.g. sleeping rough or in improvised dwellings).
- Secondary homelessness is experienced by people who frequently move from one temporary shelter to another (e.g. emergency accommodation, youth refuges, 'couch surfing').
- Tertiary homelessness is experienced by people staying in accommodation that falls below minimum community standards (e.g. boarding housing and caravan parks).

The diversity seen in the various types of inadequate housing is mirrored by the diversity in the types of individuals who seek shelter. *The Big Issue* has compiled statistics from various sources that relate to the characteristics of homeless people and highlight the diversity of the people within this group. They have found that 56% of the homeless are male, compared to 44% female; 34% have experienced domestic violence; 66% suffer from drug and alcohol abuse and up to 75% experience mental health issues. Half of all homeless people are under the age of 24 years, with 17% between the ages of 12 and 17 years. This defies the notion that the homeless are just old men living on the streets.

Various **terminology is used by the community to describe the group** called the homeless. When we think of terminology used to describe this group, it is mostly limited to *negative terminology*, which has an *impact on individuals within the group*, and links to the lack of overall support or community support for this group. Negative terms used to describe this group may include 'failures', 'bums', 'lazy', 'uneducated', 'disassociated' and 'disconnected'. Terms such as 'unkempt', 'smelly', 'homeless', 'scary' and 'drunks' are often associated with the visible homeless person living on the streets, and these terms reinforce the lack of community support . Those who are trying to support this group may describe them as 'victims', 'helpless' and 'in desperate need of help'. The impact of this terminology will differ for many people.

Sample examination questions: Multiple choice

6   A student has conducted research on homelessness in Australia and
has graphed the results, as shown.

Reasons for Homelessness In Australia

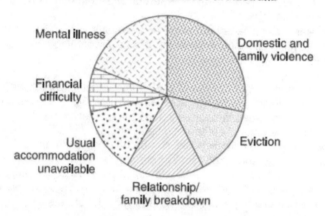

According to the student's graph, what are the most likely reasons for
homelessness in Australia?
(A) Eviction, domestic and family violence
(B) Domestic and family violence, mental illness
(C) Relationship/family breakdown, financial difficulty
(D) Usual accommodation unavailable, financial difficulty
(BOS, 2013)

7   **Which description best describes a homeless person?**
(A) Living in shared housing
(B) Living in temporary housing
(C) No access to adequate housing
(D) Inadequate access to safe and secure housing
(Adapted from BOS, 2011)

Sample examination question: Short answer

4   **What determines whether an individual is considered a homeless
person?** (2 marks)

There are many factors that determine whether a person is homeless, however
the most common theme is that a person is considered homeless if they do not
have access to safe and secure housing. This may mean they are sleeping on
friends' couches, in unstable accommodation such as boarding houses or in
between refuges. This does not mean that they are just sleeping rough and on
the streets, although this definition will include rough sleepers as well.

Issues of concern

Students learn about:	Students learn to:

issues of concern for the four specific groups within the community
satisfaction of needs
• specific needs of each group (HE SEAS)
  – health
  – education
  – safety and security
  – employment
  – adequate standard of living (food, clothing, shelter)
  – sense of identity
	• identify and prioritise the specific needs of each group
	
	• justify the TWO most significant needs for each group and discuss the implications if these are not met

access to services
• types of services, e.g. financial support, transport, accommodation and housing, health care, counselling, education, employment, legal aid
• factors affecting access to services (CAR)
  – characteristics of individuals within the group, e.g. age, gender, level of education, culture, type of disability, first language spoken, socioeconomic status
  – aspects of the service, e.g. opening hours, confidentiality, location, staffing
  – resources, e.g. time, money, energy, knowledge
	• explore the factors that can affect each group's access to services by considering the following questions:
	  – what types of services does each group require access to?
	  – how do the characteristics of individuals within each group affect their access to services?
	  – what resources are necessary to support each group's access to the service?
	  – how available are the services within the community?

Revision summary

There are **issues of concern for** the homeless including *satisfaction of needs* and *access to services*.

The *satisfaction of needs* is an issue of concern. **These specific needs** have to be *prioritised* and *justified* and all of them have *implications if these are not met*.

Health needs: These needs will differ for this group, depending on their level of shelter. For rough sleepers, health and hygiene can become an issue because of their incapacity to maintain accommodation. Up to 75% have a mental illness (*The Big Issue* statistics), which can lead to self-harm, injury and other addictions such as drug and alcohol abuse. Many homeless people would use the emergency department in hospitals for treatment, and may not go until the problem gets out of hand, causing further complications.

Employment needs: Meeting these needs can be difficult. Navigating the government's 'Work for the Dole' scheme can be difficult. Creating resumes, using technology and keeping appointments to apply for jobs are barriers to successful employment. For some, the reason for their homelessness may be the loss of employment. The *Big Issue* magazine creates employment and regular access to money to pay for rent and food.

Security and safety needs: This need is essential to fulfil for this group, but because of each individual's circumstances, it may be one of the most difficult to fulfil. This group is vulnerable without safe and secure housing and may never have this need met. Finding and establishing secure housing can be difficult due to long public housing waiting lists. The government provides funding through the Department of Housing, which creates crisis housing and other short-term housing options, but it unfortunately turns away large numbers of people waiting to access their service, increasing their vulnerability. For rough sleepers, being visible on the streets means that they are more at risk of violence and attacks. They may be vulnerable to the outside elements – long hot summers and cold winters – which can lead to health issues. Again, mental health problems and addiction problems may also be the cause of this need not being met. Impairment by drugs and alcohol can lead to risk-taking behaviour and poor decision-making leading to further problems, including those with the law.

Education: The immediate educational needs for this group may relate to knowledge of local support groups, which can support their immediate needs. Gaining access to formal schooling maybe difficult without a formal address.

Adequate standard of living needs: This need is considered a priority for the group. They are part of this minority group because they have a standard of living below the general community. Accessing shelter becomes difficult with the current housing affordability and increasing rent prices. The instability of moving between family and friends' accommodation, boarding houses (many of which are considered overcrowded and unsafe), crisis accommodation and living on the streets, make this need for this group difficult to meet. Accessing adequate food and clothing can also become an issue; under the Vagrancy Act, begging is illegal and this group can be detained if caught begging. Thus, education and gaining the knowledge of where to get free food is essential. Many charity groups provide such support.

Sense of identity: This need is the ability to understand who you are, and it can be formed around the roles you play. Being seen by society but treated as invisible will lead to a lack of identity. With no stable address and often a lack of employment, establishing where you fit into society can be extremely difficult. Without the understanding of who you are, having the confidence to seek help and accept support may lead to this need remaining unsatisfied.

Access to services is also an issue of concern for the homeless and includes **types of services** and **factors affecting access to services**.

Types of services include aspects such as financial support, transport, accommodation and housing, health care, counselling, education, employment and legal aid. Many services are <u>available</u> to this group. However, there are also many factors affecting access to these services. The major supports for this group are welfare agencies. Due to the nature of this group, seeking support can be difficult. Traumatic circumstances or personal failures may have led an individual to become homeless and because of this, formal support will need to provide a variety of services.

<u>Financial support services</u> are limited for the homeless. Centrelink payments are available for financial assistance for all Australians experiencing disadvantage, but accessing these payments can be difficult. No fixed address and a lack of identification increase the difficulty in accessing this support. However, Centrelink provides homeless outreach through community engagement officers who move around emergency housing centres. They support this group through the process and enable them to gain some financial support. Changes to the 'Work for the Dole' scheme have become another barrier to support.

<u>Transport</u>: Many homeless people move or relocate to areas where there are more services. In areas where there are higher proportions of services, transport may not be needed and walking becomes a common option. For rough sleepers, public transport may be used as a shelter to keep free from the harsh elements, however the implications of using this service is that it becomes costly. Without a costly OPAL in NSW, this group is more vulnerable to on-the-spot fines for fair evasion.

<u>Accommodation and housing</u>: Housing NSW provides emergency temporary accommodation in low-cost hotels, motels, caravan parks and suchlike for people who are or homeless or experience a housing crisis. In order to access these housing/shelter options, this group should contact Link2home. This is the new, statewide homelessness information and referral telephone service. This service is available 24 hours, 7 days per week. Accessing support is different state by state, so despite homelessness being a national issue, there are many different approaches.

<u>Health care services</u>: Health care usually comes from doctors in the emergency departments in public hospitals. This can increase the strain on already stretched resources. Bulk billing medical centres can also provide support, however, accessing a Medicare card may affect access. Emergency housing centres like the 'Oasis shelter' may provide basic first aid, however, they can make referrals to seek health care, such as calling ambulances.

<u>Counselling</u>: Relationship breakdown is one of the major reasons for homelessness. Counselling services for the homeless may not appear like counselling for the rest of the community. Communicating to welfare agencies while seeking other services, such as housing, will provide advice and strategies for this group. Welfare agencies can also provide referrals to drug and alcohol counselling and for programs to break the cycle of abuse, as well as referrals for mental health care.

Education: There is a strong association between homelessness and withdrawal from education. There are programs offered to young homeless people such as those run by the Foyer group. This formal support offers accommodation and supported living, which means young people can focus on their education – the core of this support. This type of accommodation begins with a 'something-for-something' deal, which means that the support will be provided only while the young person engages in education, in the hope that it provides young people with opportunities to develop career aspirations, to gain an experience of work, to build their networks and to build a pathway to sustainable employment. Other welfare agencies provide support for the group to become educated, however, the individual determines their success rate.

Employment: These services are essential to break the homelessness cycle. Employment services are usually linked to welfare agencies such as the Salvation Army, Mission Australia, the Wesley Mission and St Vincent de Paul. These services provide support with resume writing, interview skills, free telephones to make appointments, free internet access, support for local jobs, and support with looking appropriate for interviews, such as clean clothes and haircuts.

Legal aid: Homeless Outreach Legal Service and Homeless Persons Legal Services are both examples legal aid services. These and other similar services offer drop-in access to free legal advice and representation. The homeless group may experience trouble with the law for many reasons such as fair evasion, begging, loitering in a public place or starting a fire for warmth.

Factors affecting access to services can be remembered by the acronym CAR. Characteristics of individuals within the group; e.g. first language spoken, culture, socioeconomic status, type of disability, age, gender, level of education (Lights. Camera. STAGE); aspects of the service, e.g. location, opening hours, confidentiality, staffing (LOCS); and resources, e.g. KEMT.

The individual characteristics of a homeless person may influence their access to services. The age of the individual may determine if they can access a service. Many services target women and young people, leaving older homeless people to compete for the available services directed at them. Age may influence societal attitudes towards the group; members of the community may dismiss the needs of young homeless people, feeling that they are young enough to go home and are simply not conforming to their parents' rules. As previously said, many services are targeted towards women and young people, however, statistics show that there are more homeless males (56%, ABS). This may limit the male homeless population from breaking the homeless cycle. Therefore, a person's gender may influence their access to these services. The culture and first language spoken of an individual may limit an individual's ability to communicate or fully partake in the services that formal agencies provide. It is estimated that 30% (Homelessness Australia) of homeless people are born overseas while 25% are Aboriginal and Torres Strait Islander. Being culturally sensitive and having access to an interpreter will increase the likelihood of access to these supports. This group's low socioeconomic status (SES) is a key factor in the homeless cycle from generation to generation. A low SES is a key determinant for the inclusion in this group. For those with a higher SES would just pay for rental accommodation or housing, thus many supports that are available to the low SES group are free or low-cost. However, if an individual is to break free from the homelessness cycle, ultimately they will need to improve their SES. An individual's level of education may influence their knowledge of local support services, their ability to complete complicated forms for rental and financial support applications and even their level of skill to gain employment. Level of education may be influenced by a disability. For those without a disability accessing services can be extremely difficult; having a disability makes access even more difficult. The type of disability will influence the support needed. For those with mental health issues, behaviours associated with mental illness may increase the discrimination against this group. For those with a physical disability, finding appropriate emergency housing that can accommodate them limits the services available.

Aspects of the service will dictate whether a person can access it. Despite a service being available for use, if a service's opening hours are not suitable for when the individual needs it, the service will not be used. Services for this group need to be available 24 hours per day. Instances of individuals fleeing from domestic violence incidences most commonly occur outside general opening times. An individual will not use a service if the location is too far away. As discussed earlier, accessing public transport is costly, and many of the homeless community rely on walking. This group relies on the confidentiality of a service. Many victims leaving a violent home or sexual abuse fear their perpetrator may find them and force them back into the situation they left. It is essential that the staff in support services targeting this group are trained and show compassion and patience. If an individual has a negative experience with staff at a service, it may mean that they stop seeking support.

A lack of resources is another factor affecting access to services. There is a severe lack of resources available to support the homeless. This, coupled with the lack of resources that the individual may experience, may mean that homelessness is experienced for long periods. Despite the perceived notion that the homeless have large amounts of time, they may spend a large proportion of it waiting for services: waiting to see if there is a bed available, waiting for meals to be served, waiting to hear if they have appointments for potential accommodation or employment and so on. As resources are stretched, staffing numbers are limited and this group will spend time waiting for their turn while the need is high. A large proportion of the day will be spent in seeking shelter for the night and determining where they will get food. Everything else is secondary to these essential standard of living needs. When nutritional food sources are low, this group will not receive the energy they need to fulfil daily tasks. Knowledge as a resource is essential to daily survival for this group. Without money to pay for shelter and food, energy is spent on trying to find these resources for survival.

Sample examination questions: Multiple choice

8   Which of the following would most improve the security and safety needs of a homeless family?
(A) Centrelink
(B) Parents without partners
(C) St Vincent de Paul
(D) Family and of Community Services
(Adapted from BOSTES, 2014)

9   Chris is a 16-year-old boy living on the streets of Sydney.
     Which of the following would most affect his access to resources?
(A) Age, knowledge and aspects of the service
(B) Employment, education and age
(C) Confidentiality, legal aid and health care
(D) Disability, location and knowledge
(Adapted from BOS, 2012)

10   Which of the following needs is satisfied most when a person is
     provided with access to affordable housing?
(A) Health
(B) Employment
(C) Sense of identity
(D) Adequate standard of living
(Adapted from BOS, 2011)

Sample examination questions: Short answer

5   Compare ONE significant need for both the HOMELESS and for
     PEOPLE WITH A DISABILITY. (3 marks)

Security and safety needs are a significant need for both of these groups; they
are both vulnerable to outside people, as threats may come in the form of injury,
however the risks influencing security and safety differ.

Homeless who live on the streets are vulnerable because they are so evident.
Their security and safety needs are threatened because they have no shelter;
they are at risk of illness and skin infections due to harsh weather conditions, as
well as being at risk of attack and predatory behaviour from the public. This
differs to people with a disability. This group is vulnerable due to aspects of their
disability. For those with a sensory disability, they may be prone to falls or injury
as they may not see an object or cannot navigate an area within the community.
For those with an intellectual disability with a developmental delay, people within
the community may prey on their weakness, which is a similar situation to the
homeless. Predatory people may take advantage, thinking that they can exploit
the delay in understanding of those with an intellectual disability.

6   Homeless people have significant needs.
     Select TWO of their most significant needs and justify your choice.
     (4 marks) (Adapted from BOS, 2010)

Adequate standard of living skills: (ASoL). The homeless group is defined by their
lack of adequate shelter; therefore ASoL (food, clothing and shelter) needs are
their most specific. Without adequate shelter, adequate clothing and food it is
difficult to survive. This group relies on community support to meet these needs,
as they do not have the means, i.e. employment (begging is illegal under the
Vagrancy Act), or resources (financial support) to fulfil this need themselves.

Safety and security: Rough sleepers are vulnerable as they are very visible in the community. Asking the community for food or money opens this group up to the risk of negative language and abuse reflecting community attitudes. Rough sleepers may be fleeing domestic violence with their children and they may be in hiding from a dangerous partner, therefore increasing their risks and their need to stay in hiding, which may limit them seeking support. Rough sleepers will also sleep outside and are exposed to the elements. Hypothermia or hyperthermia (freezing or overheating) risks this group's medical safety, which may lead to acute illness. As 66% of the homeless have an addiction, this group's decision-making skills maybe impaired, therefore putting their security and safety at risk.

Category B: Youth

<table>
<tr>
<td colspan="2">
Category B groups
(Select two groups)
<ul>
<li>Aged</li>
<li>Culturally and Linguistically Diverse communities</li>
<li>Aboriginal and Torres Strait Islander peoples</li>
<li>Rural and remote families</li>
<li>Gay, Lesbian, Bisexual, Transgender, Intersex communities</li>
<li>Sole parents</li>
<li>Youth</li>
</ul>
</td>
</tr>
<tr>
<td>Students learn about:</td>
<td>Students learn to:</td>
</tr>
<tr>
<td>
exploring the four specific groups within the community
<ul>
<li>prevalence of each group within the community</li>
<li>individual diversity within each group</li>
<li>terminology used by the community to describe the group</li>
</ul>
</td>
<td>
<ul>
<li>utilise reliable sources of data to examine the nature of each group by considering the following questions:
  <ul>
  <li>– what is the prevalence of the group within Australia?</li>
  <li>– what determines whether an individual is part of the group?</li>
  <li>– how might individuals vary within the group?</li>
  </ul>
</li>
<li>recognise that the community uses positive and negative terminology to describe each group. Discuss the impact this might have on individuals within the group</li>
</ul>
</td>
</tr>
</table>

Revision summary

When **exploring** youth **within the community** it is essential to look at the **prevalence of the group within the community**, **individual diversity within each group** and **terminology used by the community to describe the group.**

The factor that <u>determines whether an individual is part of the group</u> is their age. According to The United Nations General Assembly, youth is defined as those persons falling between the ages of 15 and 24 years. The 2010 National Strategy for Young Australians defines youth in general as 12–24 years of age. Similarly, the study *Young Australians: their health and wellbeing* (2011) carried out by the Australian Institute of Health and Welfare (AIHW) also defines young people as aged 12–24 years.

The prevalence of youth within the community includes the fact that there were 4 280 322 persons between the age of 12 to 25 in Australia in 2013. This was 18.6% of the population (McCrindle Research, 2013). Males made up 51.3% and females made up the remaining 48.7% (McCrindle Research, 2013). Due to lower birth rates and a decline in fertility, the youth population is predicted to decrease from 19.4% in 2008 to under 18% in 2020 (McCrindle Research, 2013). Eight per cent of young people aged 15–24 had some form of disability (ABS, 2013).

The individual diversity of youth is marked by the various milestones that exist within the group, ranging from puberty, to age of consent, adulthood, continuation of education, entry into training, full-time employment, moving out of home, buying/renting a house, marriage and possibly child rearing. Individual youths might vary within the group due to different personal, family, cultural, religious, education and workplace roles and responsibilities.

Terminology used by the community to describe youth is often reflective of the milestones or experiences. Positive terminology might include terms like 'fun loving', 'carefree', 'future generation', 'adolescent', 'teenager' and 'young person'. This type of terminology might <u>impact on individuals within the group</u> in a positive way, as youth may feel appreciated and valued for their contribution to the community. Negative terminology might include 'bludgers', 'nuisance', 'trouble makers', 'rebellious', 'geek', 'lad', 'grommet', 'emo', 'goth', 'risk-taker' or other possible derogatory terms used to describe certain individual diversities of youths. This type of terminology may have a detrimental <u>impact on individuals within the group</u> in terms of lowering self-esteem and self-identity and it could cause youths to rebel or cease to contribute to the community.

Sample examination questions: Short answer

7   **How might individuals vary within ONE group you have studied**? (4 marks)

NB: You can insert either of the category A group or any of the category B groups you have studied.

> Group: Youth

Individual diversity within the youth group varies considerably. Youth is defined by The United Nations General Assembly (2014) as those persons falling between the ages of 15 and 24 years.

Within this age bracket there are various areas of diversity, by which one can differentiate each youth. Some younger youths such as those between 15 and 18 years of age are still undergoing formal education, most of which takes place at a mainstream school or, in special circumstances, TAFE or an alternative learning environment such as the type offered by Marist Youth Care at Pete's Place, Blacktown. Youths in this age bracket are either well into the stage of puberty or, for some males in particular, only just starting to experience the many changes associated with this stage of life. Some may work part-time and may be involved in various after school sporting and leisure activities, as well as possibly engage in community service activities.

Between the ages of 18 and 21 many youths are either studying at TAFE, college, university or are employed in entry-level positions. Those who are studying attempt to balance their multiple commitments by working and studying, with many youths choosing to defer their educational payments. Some youths within this particular bracket may be travelling the world, relying on savings from part-time work, money from their parents or any casual work they might be able to acquire. There may be a small number of youths attempting to trial living outside of the family home, but there is a trend for many youths to live at home well into their late twenties.

Youths in the latter part of the group such as those who are 21–24 years of age are possibly starting to consider career prospects, with many attempting to gain full-time employment. Some youths are successful and receive full-time contracts, but a large number of youths are either engaged in casual or part-time work in low-paying jobs or are unemployed. Many youths may also be starting to form close bonds with a partner and may consider their future together with this person. This could be through moving in together and possibly getting engaged.

Issues of concern

Students learn about:	Students learn to:

issues of concern for the four specific groups within the community
satisfaction of needs
• specific needs of each group
  – adequate standard of living (food, clothing, shelter)
  – health
  – education
  – employment
  – safety and security
  – sense of identity
access to services
• types of services, e.g. financial support, transport, accommodation and housing, health care, counselling, education, employment, legal aid
• factors affecting access to services
  – characteristics of individuals within the group, e.g. age, gender, level of education, culture, type of disability, first language spoken, socioeconomic status
  – resources, e.g. time, money, energy, knowledge
  – aspects of the service, e.g. opening hours, confidentiality, location, staffing
	• identify and prioritise the specific needs of each group
	• justify the TWO most significant needs for each group and discuss the implications if these are not met
	
	• explore the factors that can affect each group's access to services by considering the following questions:
	  – what types of services does each group require access to?
	  – how do the characteristics of individuals within each group affect their access to services?
	  – what resources are necessary to support each group's access to the service?
	  – how available are the services within the community?

Revision summary

The **issues of concern** for youth include *satisfaction of needs* and *access to services*.

The *satisfaction of needs* is an issue of concern and includes specific needs of each group such as HESEAS – <u>health</u>, <u>education</u>, <u>safety and security</u>, <u>employment</u>, <u>adequate standard of living (food, clothing, shelter)</u> and <u>sense of identity</u>. These specific needs to have to be *prioritised* and *justified* and all of them have *implications if these are not met.*

Youth are in a vulnerable stage of life and their <u>health</u> is of importance to their overall wellbeing. Nutrition and appropriate health care is important for their rapid growth and development, especially at a stage when they also need energy for participation in sport/recreation and education. Medicare can be accessed by individuals after 15 years of age. Private health insurance may be taken out for injuries sustained during risk-taking behaviour such as alcohol or drug use, unsafe driving or sport/leisure. It could also be required for procedures common at that stage of life, such as dental work, i.e. braces or wisdom teeth removal. Drug, alcohol, driving, eating behaviour, mental health, travel and safe sex awareness is imperative for this specific group.

Education is a specific need that has to be satisfied by youths. Schooling allows youths to gain foundational knowledge and skills for their future in literacy, numeracy, health, social sciences, technology and the arts. In addition to this is the valuable life and work skills embedded into many of the subjects, all of which make education even more important for youth. Youth are required by Australian law to stay at school until 17 years of age and as a result many youths are staying on to complete their HSC or equivalent. These sorts of certificates give youths more choice and a pathway into further education in TAFEs, colleges and universities. This then provides youth with an opportunity to study and then apply the knowledge and skills developed. Upon completing a course, education does not stop for youth, but continues throughout their working life.

The safety and security of youths is a significant need due to their exploration and experimentation. In terms of safety, youths need to ensure they are engaging in safe behaviours in relationships, sport/leisure, school and work. Safety in a physical sense sees youths gaining knowledge about staying safe in many different scenarios. Safety and security in terms of technology is also important for youth as developing and practising strategies for safe technology use is essential. Personal security can take the form of travelling in large groups instead of alone and making informed choices about drug and alcohol use, eating behaviours, relationship decisions and technology habits. Security can also include the need for youths to socialise and interact in groups. Another factor is financial stability, which youth often do not have.

In terms of employment, youths spend a fair amount of time creating opportunities for their future: attending school to develop work and enterprise skills, participating in casual employment and then possibly working part-time while studying. After graduating from high school or higher education, youths may start off volunteering or doing work experience or go straight into entry-level jobs, which are often temporary, and there may be no guarantee of permanency. Youths in today's community may have several career changes in their lives.

The adequate standard of living for many youths may mean that they still have shelter by residing with their parents or guardians well into their late 20s. During this time many may be employed in full-time work and as a result are required to pay board, contribute financially and/or complete household duties in the family home. Some youths decide to rent with friends or their partners, but often return home to save money for overseas travel, further education costs or to purchase their first home or rental. Some parents/guardians still pay for and choose food for their youth, although many seek assistance from them to prepare and clean up after family meals. During this time youth may make poor food choices, often resorting to meals and drinks that are convenient and have a low nutritional value as they are busy managing their multiple roles of studying and attempting to work. Clothing choices are made predominately by youths, but often parents/guardians may not agree with the price associated with designer labels or the latest fashion. These choices are often linked to their sense of identity, self-esteem and status.

Access to services for youth includes the types of services and factors affecting access to services for youth.

Types of services youth *require access to* may include:

Type of service	Examples
Financial support	Youth Allowance, Newstart, ABSTUDY and Disability Support Pension from Centrelink, Study Assist, NSW Photo Cards for leisure activity concessions.
Transport	School Student Transport Scheme for discounted travel to and from school, School Term Bus Pass, Senior Secondary Student Concession Card, NSW Tertiary Student Concession Card, YASS and YAXI.
Accommodation and housing	Youth Solutions, Youth Off The Streets, St Vincent de Paul, Youth Housing and crisis accommodation offered through a variety of services.
Health care	Medicare card, private health insurance under parents/guardians up until 25 years, PBS and Child Dental Benefits Schedule.
Counselling	Catholic Care, Anglicare, headspace, Kid's Helpline, Lifeline, Reach Out and Beyond Blue.
Education	Private or public schools, distance education, online courses, universities, TAFES, colleges and tutoring, pathways.
Employment	Careers advisors in schools, TAFES and universities, Australian Apprenticeships, Job Services Australia and Youth Employment Services, Links to Learning, Youth Connections.
Legal aid	Children's Legal Service of Legal Aid NSW and The Shopfront Legal Centre.

The characteristics of individuals may **affect access to services** for youth. First language spoken may impact access for youth, as some services may only be available in certain languages, creating language barriers. Similar to this is culture where there may be cultural restrictions that prevent youth accessing particular services.

A youth's socioeconomic status may affect what services they access. Services that incur significant costs and are further distances away may inhibit this group's access as they have less disposable income available and may be embarrassed to access. The type of disability of a youth may further limit their access to services, possibly due to physical restrictions, their mental state or lowered self-esteem. The age of a youth may impact on the choice in services available due to physical location, eligibility and possibly a lack of confidence for younger youths. Gender may be another factor that affects the type of service, as some are gender based. Many young males are also reluctant to access services to support their needs. Level of education may impact youth in terms of awareness and exposure of services due difficulties either understanding or accessing the information.

How available the services are within the community includes aspects of the service such as location, opening hours, confidentiality and staffing. The location of a service may make it physically difficult to access services due to costs of public transport or rural/remoteness. In addition, there may not be enough availability of particular services if the demand is too high due to population and needs of youth in certain areas. Services may have specific opening hours that might not be in sync with youth while they are busy either at school, studying, working or assisting their family. Often the opening hours reflect a traditional working day to suit the employees rather than the needs of youth. Some youth may be so wary of the level of confidentiality offered by certain services that they simply do not access them. Finally, the gender, religion, culture, demeanour, availability or lack of staff may impact on the access of youth to services.

The *resources necessary to support youth's access to services* include knowledge, energy, money and time. Resources such as knowledge may affect access to services as there may be a lack of understanding or awareness that certain services exist, especially free services. Many youths often lack the energy or motivation to investigate services. Some could also be quite tired physically from trying to manage their multiple roles in study, work and family. Money becomes an issue when accessing some services for youth due to extensive costs of access or they may not be able to access certain subsidised services as they or their parents earn too much. Time also links with motivation, but some youths are too busy enjoying leisure time or working hard to have a life balance so they simply do not feel they have the time to invest in accessing appropriate services.

Sample examination questions: Short answer

8   **Justify the TWO most significant needs for ONE group you have studied.** (6 marks)

NB: You can insert either of the category A group or any of the category B groups you have studied.

Group: Youth

There are various needs that can be satisfied and prioritised to indicate the most important requirements for the wellbeing of youths at their particular stage of life. Two needs that are highly significant are health and education.

Health is extremely critical for youth at this stage of life and it is essential for their overall wellbeing. Due to the rapid physical growth that youths are experiencing during this stage of their lives, nutrition is essential in providing them with the key nutrients for their bodies to grow and develop. Many youths undergo growth spurts, which can be associated with the need for foods that satisfy their hunger, as well as provide enough energy for their active bodies. For this reason, it can be argued that healthy food choices need to also be made because of the brain development and learning that many youths are experiencing during schooling, in further education or at the start of their careers. Youths also need to make wise personal choices and limit their risk of unsafe health behaviours such as unsafe sexual intercourse, drink driving, self-harm or dangerous technology use. There is evidence to suggest that the choices and decisions made in this stage of life are critical to the paths that their lives may take in the early stages of adulthood and beyond.

In addition, education is a significant need for youths at this stage of their lives. Many youths are engaging in formal schooling during this time and knowledge gained is key to the success and accomplishment of important skills in literacy, numeracy, health, social science, technology and the arts for the future. Embedded into many aspects of schooling are valuable work and enterprise skills as well as principles for youths to become valued citizens of the community. It is during this stage of life that youth are also starting to prepare for their future after formal, compulsory education. This is evidence as to why education is a highly significant need for youth at this stage of life. Youths need to start exploring and researching possible future directions and to start to set goals for themselves about what their future career might look like and how they can get it. This is not to say that education ceases after formal schooling, but it is the key to a successful and satisfying career.

Creating positive social environments

Students learn about:	Students learn to:
creating positive social environments *addressing the groups' issues of concern* • government policy and legislation • organisations within the community that support the group • equity issues	• examine government policy and legislation to determine its role in ensuring equity for each group • critically analyse the extent to which organisations within the community assist in satisfying the needs of each group • investigate a current inequity issue faced by each group and propose strategies to address the issue

Revision summary

Positive social environments at home, school, work and leisure can be created for youth by *addressing the groups' issues of concern*. This can occur through government policy and legislation, organisations within the community that support the group and by addressing equity issues.

Government policy and legislation plays an important role in *ensuring equity for youth*. Policies such as *The Children and Young Persons (Care and Protection) Act 1998, Child Protection (Working with Children) Act 2012, Young Offenders Act 1997, Age Discrimination Act 2004*, Convention on the Rights of the Child, The Education Amendment Bill 2009 (NSW), *Marriage Act 1961 (Cwlth) NSW*, Youth Allowance, ABSTUDY and concessions for public transport are all examples of policies and regulations that ensure equity for youth in various ways.

Within Australia, there are numerous organisations within the community that support youth. They all have different functions and *assist in satisfying the needs of* youth to a minor and major extent. Some include: The Children's Hospital Westmead, Kids Help Line, Centrelink, Lighthouse, WEAVE, The Reach Foundation, PCYC, Sydney Youth Services, Youth off the Street, Youth Action, Salvos Youth Network, Wesley Youth Services and Twenty 10.

Equity issues include issues around justice and equality that may be experienced. Various *inequity issues faced by* youth within the greater community include: the right to vote, driving and drinking restrictions, financial issues, harassment and discrimination, negative terminology to describe the group, permanent employment, health services and educational inequities.

Strategies to address the issue could be developed to ensure fairness and a sense of justice.

Sample examination questions: Short answer

9 **Propose strategies that can be implemented to address a current inequity issue faced by ONE of the groups listed below:** (8 marks) (Adapted from BOSTES, 2014)

- Aged
- Culturally and Linguistically Diverse communities
- Aboriginal and Torres Strait Islander peoples
- Rural and remote families
- Gay, Lesbian, Bisexual, Transgender and Intersex communities
- Sole parents
- Youth

Group: Youth

According to UNESCO (2016), youth can be defined as those persons falling between the ages of 15 and 24 years of age. Youth are often disadvantaged members of the community and experience many inequalities due to a number of factors surrounding their age and characteristics.

One such inequity issue is the unemployment/underemployment many youths face where they are often employed in entry-level positions for sustained periods and there is a reduced number of full-time positions offered to graduate recruits.

From an educational level, strategies to reduce this inequity issue is to create opportunities for senior students and even undergraduates to be further supported in their transition to employment. Participating in compulsory and meaningful work experience could assist in this area. Training courses such as first aid, WHS and white cards offered by schools, TAFE or university levels by trained facilitators may also contribute to reducing this inequity.

Another potential solution is offering different modes of educational delivery and alternative options for youths not coping or benefitting from mainstream schooling so they can engage in education, training and transition into the workforce. Opening up distance education for those students with diagnosed mental health illnesses would allow affected youths to access formal education within the home, therefore possibly aiding the improvement of the inequity issue of unemployment/underemployment.

Another appropriate strategy to address this issue is for organisations to sponsor graduating recruits in all industries. By sponsoring these individuals, recruits may have a greater chance of receiving full-time contracts as they have worked closely with the organisation prior to employment. Universities may also contribute part of this sponsorship through incentives, training and monetary support, resulting in more offers of employment.

Organisations may also have access to various government incentives and schemes for employing graduating recruits in full-time positions. By increasing monetary incentives for employers to take on graduating recruits and apprentices in trades, or even creating legislation creating compulsory apprenticeships for each business, it makes employing graduates or apprentices more attractive for employers. Other incentives could include discounted costs of insurance, reduced business registration or free training programs to support the youths who are newly employed.

In addition, another strategy that may reduce the financial disadvantage experienced by youth in unemployment/underemployment could be mentoring/coaching programs offered to businesses/organisations and their teams for taking on newly appointed youths. Training could be run in-house to reduce the financial burden on the government. This mentoring/coaching may mean that there are greater opportunities for youth full-time employment as the new recruits are closely monitored and developed from within the organisation.

The implementation of such strategies may assist in reducing the unemployment/underemployment rates and financial disadvantages that currently exists for Australian youths.

10 Assess the extent to which organisations within the community assist in satisfying the needs of TWO of the groups listed below: (8 marks) (Adapted from BOS, 2013)

- Aged
- Culturally and Linguistically Diverse communities
- Aboriginal and Torres Strait Islander peoples
- Rural and remote families
- Gay, Lesbian, Bisexual, Transgender and Intersex communities
- Sole parents
- Youth

Groups: Youth and Aged

Organisations within the community can assist in satisfying the needs of youth and aged to either a major or moderate extent.

Kids Help Line may have a profound impact on the health and safety and security needs of youth as it is a free service, easily accessible online and via telephone, and it is available 24 hours a day every day of the year. On the other hand, due to the high demand of the free service, youths may experience waiting times, as there could be a shortage of staff available to speak with them. An alternative option is Catholic Care Counselling, which may incur costs calculated based on household income; however, all fees are negotiable and their policy is not to refuse their service if youths are unable to pay. Youths may be reluctant to seek help from a religious organisation, as they may be worried that they may be judged, or their need for counselling may surround issues such as sexuality and premarital sexual behaviour that this religion does not support.

headspace is another organisation within the community that supports the health and safety and security needs of youth. There are more than 80 services available nationally across metropolitan, regional and rural areas of Australia for youth. headspace can be accessed through headspace centres, online counselling services, eheadspace and headspace School Support. Their service may be at times difficult to access, as there are some low fees charged and some services require referrals from a doctor, therefore limiting the extent to which this organisation assists in satisfying the needs of youth. The eheadspace online space creates an excellent method of reaching youth and supporting them with their needs. With youth being technologically savvy, this method supports the health needs of those youth in rural or isolated areas, those who have a low socioeconomic status and those who may be having sense of identity issues due to their sexuality.

St Vincent de Paul Youth Housing offer an adequate standard of living through clean, safe, affordable and subsidised housing open to young people who are homeless or at risk of being homeless irrespective of their background. 'Vinnies' work with youths to improve their living skills, encourage them to engage in education and return to their family home. This assists in satisfying the health (clean, safe and hygienic) and security and safety (offering staffed housing) needs of youth to a major extent.

Organisations within the community that help satisfy the health and security and safety needs of aged include beyondblue's program Life Starts at Sixty, Connections resources and Meals on Wheels. Life Starts at Sixty has a variety of online resources and links for aged individuals suffering depression and anxiety. It includes two real-life stories from aged individuals, signs and symptoms information and an extensive booklet called *Connections*. The organisation would support aged individuals to a moderate extent as although it has a variety of resources available, which could help satisfy the health and sense of identity needs of aged individuals, it does not provide direct counselling and support, merely links to various resources and information.

Meals on Wheels is a national service that offers a meal (nutrition), a safety and wellbeing check (monitoring of physical and psychological wellbeing) and social cohesiveness (strengthening communities/locals helping locals) to individuals who are frail, aged and may have a disability. Meals on Wheels has services that span the country through metropolitan, regional and rural areas, often delivered by volunteers. The fact that they offer a whole range of services and actions that can support the health and sense of identity needs of aged individuals makes it one of the organisations that support aged individuals to a major extent.

Men's Shed and Older Women's Network are organisations that support the sense of identity needs for aged individuals, based on gender. Both organisations provide opportunities for aged individuals to share experiences and work on meaningful projects, initiatives and activities. These organisations support the sense of identity needs of aged to a major extent, through participation in government lobbying, involvement in wellness and health seminars, networking opportunities, advocacy and community participation. Daily involvement in these programs will create a sense of purpose, meaning and a reason to be an active community member – all contributing to the sense of identity. Involvement in these also contributes successfully to safety and security needs, as the informal support networks created by these organisations means there is someone to check on the safety of individuals regularly.

Positive influences of community attitudes

Students learn about:	Students learn to:

positive influences on community attitudes
 • contributions the group makes within the community
 • advocacy (speaking up for the group's needs and concerns)
   – raising awareness within the community
   – educating the community
   – promoting the rights of the group
	• explore ONE example of what each group has done to try to improve community attitudes, and assess the impact this has had on the wellbeing of the group
	 • outline how community organisations advocate for each group and describe the positive influence it can have on community attitudes

Revision summary

The *positive influences on community attitudes* in terms of what youth have done to try to improve community attitudes stem from <u>contributions youth make within the community</u> and *how community organisations advocate* for youth.

Positive contributions made by youth have an *impact on the wellbeing of* youth. Some <u>contributions youth make within the community</u> include: volunteering in positions such as babysitting, tutoring, coaching, church, emergency services and charity work; actively engaging in social media which trends issues in the community; contributing to discussions within the local community; actively involving themselves in schooling and post-school opportunities; participating in social groups such as sewing, book clubs scrapbooking, sporting teams and gyms; undertaking casual and part-time employment; caring for younger siblings or parents who need care; fundraising for various causes; capturing moments in the community; and sharing their knowledge and love of technology.

<u>Advocacy</u> (speaking up for the group's needs and concerns) is an important aspect of *improving community attitudes* towards youth. There are a large number of community organisations that have a positive influence on community attitudes. Organisations such as PCYC can <u>raise awareness</u> of youth by developing programs and various activities for youth to participate in. Another way community organisations advocate for youth is by <u>educating the community</u> by promoting positive stories of youth in the media, developing programs between aged care facilities and local high schools, sharing stories of influential youth, sharing examples of the volunteer work they might be undertaking and holding workshops on youth issues such as body image or using technology. <u>Promoting the rights of the group</u> is another way to speak up for the group's needs and concerns. Some examples may include showcasing/attending forums or workshops, Youth Ambassadors at local councils, the governance of safety and other guidelines, advertising events and issues using different platforms, government department programs or incentives, online courses/clips/fact sheets, case studies and research on youth issues, youth days, competitions and festivals and Young Australian of the Year.

Sample examination questions: Short answer

11 For ONE of the groups below, outline how community organisations advocate for the group and describe the positive influence it can have on community attitudes: (8 marks)

- Aged
- Culturally and Linguistically Diverse communities
- Aboriginal and Torres Strait Islander peoples
- Rural and remote families
- Gay, Lesbian, Bisexual, Transgender and Intersex communities
- Sole parents
- Youth

Group: Youth

There are various community organisations that advocate for youth by raising awareness, educating and/or promoting their rights. The work of these organisations can have a significant positive influence on community attitudes towards youth.

Youth Off The Streets advocates for youth by raising awareness within the community in opening up options to build mentoring opportunities with community members to help youths achieve their goals. This has a positive influence on community attitudes as community members involved can see first-hand the capacity of youths and be able to speak highly of the positive interactions they have with youths. In addition, Youth Off The Streets offers a service-learning program where youths contribute to the community by volunteering at retirement homes, animal shelters and hospitals and help to sustain community gardens. This favourable exposure of youth's contributions has a positive influence on community attitudes as it raises awareness of the group within the community by showing the commitment and dedication youths can have towards supporting the needs of others and that they can make a positive contribution to society.

Another organisation that advocates for youth is Youth Solutions, which is a youth drug and alcohol prevention and health promotion charity that works with young people and the broader community. Youth Solutions aims to educate the community about youth through developing partnerships, building capacity and supporting positive community action. These partnerships can lead to stronger relationships being developed between community members and youths and would create a positive influence on community attitudes. One such example is through their strong partnership with Campbelltown Catholic Club and other surrounding businesses in the region that have been able to assist in sharing the positive messages portrayed through projects and campaigns within the organisation. This corporate partnership would lead to further positive influences on community attitudes by bringing local businesses together, developing strong connections within the community and offering community events and activities.

Another notable organisation that advocates for youth is headspace, the National Youth Mental Health Foundation providing early intervention mental health services to 12–25 year olds. headspace promotes the rights of youth such as the right to the protection of the child's mental development, the right to seek help and the right to enjoy life with dignity and respect. These rights are promoted through the various programs and services that are offered by headspace, as well as by the numerous centres that operate around the country. headspace has a positive influence on community attitudes towards youth due to the health promotion and community awareness activities it offers, as well as the widespread corporate and community support and position papers it offers to inform the community about particular issues pertaining to youth.

Category B: Aged

<table>
<tr><td colspan="2" align="center">Category B groups
(Select two groups)
• Aged
• Culturally and Linguistically Diverse communities
• Aboriginal and Torres Strait Islander peoples
• Rural and remote families
• Gay, Lesbian, Bisexual, Transgender and Intersex communities
• Sole parents
• Youth</td></tr>
<tr><td>Students learn about:</td><td>Students learn to:</td></tr>
<tr>
<td>exploring the four specific groups within the community
• prevalence of each group within the community
• individual diversity within each group
• terminology used by the community to describe the group</td>
<td>• utilise reliable sources of data to examine the nature of each group by considering the following questions:
  – what is the prevalence of the group within Australia?
  – what determines whether an individual is part of the group?
  – how might individuals vary within the group?
• recognise that the community uses positive and negative terminology to describe each group. Discuss the impact this might have on individuals within the group</td>
</tr>
</table>

Revision summary

The aged are recognised and defined by their age. The Australian Bureau of Statistics refers to the aged as 'those individuals who are over 65 years of age'.

The **prevalence of this group within the community**, specifically *within Australia*, is represented by 14.4% of the population or approximately 3.3 million people and is the fastest growing age group in the population.

An individual's age *determines whether an individual is a part of this group*. However, people age at different rates, thus creating the **diversity amongst this group**. Physiologically, as individuals age the processes within their bodies are not working as well as they once did. The natural ageing process of the body creates messages that, when sent to the brain, are confused, sounds are muffled and not as sharp, and colours become dull. The brain has to work harder to decode the messages sent to the brain from its five senses, and with the extra time taken to decode the messages it creates the perception of confusion. The body is also working harder to move the degeneration of cartilage (soft tissue that prevents the bone from rubbing), which means that once protected bones may rub when moving, creating pain, thus movement becomes slower. These changes to the body happen at different rates for each individual.

The terminology used to describe the group can be both positive and negative. The negativity may come from frustration and a lack of understanding of what is happening in their body causing the changes to movement, personality and ability. Because of this, the aged may be referred to as 'slow', 'ancient', 'accident prone', 'aggressive', 'doddery old fools', 'grumpy old men', 'geriatrics', 'old dear' and 'gossipmongers'. When understanding is created and appreciation is given for the contribution this group make, this group are described as 'loving', 'role models', 'a wealth of knowledge and wisdom', 'irreplaceable', 'supportive', 'experienced contributors' and '100 years young'. The impact of this terminology will be different for everyone.

Sample examination questions: Short answer

12 **Discuss the impact that positive and negative terminology used to describe the group might have on individuals within the group.**
(4 marks)

The aged are those people aged more than 65 years. They are the fastest growing group in the community, and thus when describing the group, positive and negative terminology can have great effects.

When describing the aged, negative terminology relating to their abilities and personalities can have negative impacts. For those described as 'doddery old fools', 'slow', 'worst drivers', 'accidents waiting to happen, 'past their used by date', 'better off dead, 'old dear', 'ancient', 'aggressive' and 'grumpy' it can have a vast effect on their confidence. Hearing that your skills are no longer useful may cause an individual to not participate in activities that they may have taken part it. Withdrawal and social isolation is common for this group, and with community attitudes discouraging participation, this group will become dependent on society at a faster rate. The participation of this group is important, as this group are a brilliant informal support. They care for grandchildren and support the community with their volunteer work, thus they feel useful and appreciated.

When this group is appreciated within society they are often described in terms such as 'loving', 'role models', 'a wealth of knowledge and wisdom', 'irreplaceable', 'supportive', 'experienced contributors' and '100 years young'. The impact that this has is enormous for their sense of identity and their willingness to continue to contribute.

Issues of concern

Students learn about:	Students learn to:

issues of concern for the four specific groups within the community *satisfaction of needs*
 • specific needs of each group
    – adequate standard of living (food, clothing, shelter)
    – health
    – education
    – employment
    – safety and security
    – sense of identity
 access to services
 • types of services, e.g. financial support, transport, accommodation and housing, health care, counselling, education, employment, legal aid
 • factors affecting access to services
    – characteristics of individuals within the group, e.g. age, gender, level of education, culture, type of disability, first language spoken, socioeconomic status
    – resources, e.g. time, money, energy, knowledge
    – aspects of the service, e.g. opening hours, confidentiality, location, staffing
	• identify and prioritise the specific needs of each group
	
	 • justify the TWO most significant needs for each group and discuss the implications if these are not met
	
	 • explore the factors that can affect each group's access to services by considering the following questions:
	    – what types of services does each group require access to?
	    – how do the characteristics of individuals within each group affect their access to services?
	    – what resources are necessary to support each group's access to the service?
	    – how available are the services within the community?

Revision summary

There are **issues of concern for** the aged including *satisfaction of needs* and *access to services*.

The *satisfaction of needs* is an issue of concern. **These specific needs** have to be *prioritised* and *justified* and all of them have *implications if these are not met*.

The health needs of this group are a major priority. The health problems that this group experience are associated with their age and the deterioration of the body. The consequences of choices made in early life are starting to develop. Cancers, cardiovascular disease, reduced bone density, arthritis, and perhaps obesity are all common health concerns. Due to reduced mobility and less energy, this group is less likely to spend the time making healthy and nutritious meals, which may also influence their health. This group is living longer, which means health costs are likely to increase for the individual.

Education for this group is less likely to be formal learning, although some aged people do go to educational courses and some even complete their HSC! For this group, they will need to gain knowledge on meeting their own health needs. Type two diabetes can start later in life and will need a complete change of diet; learning how to choose healthy meals is important. Stimulating the mind has been linked to reducing the chances of developing Alzheimer's disease and dementia.

Security and safety for this group is important as the aged can be vulnerable in society. Their security and safety needs should be met to lower the chances of slips, falls, predators and opportunists. As the functioning of the five senses decreases, the body is less likely to register potential trip hazards, for example, long curtains, uneven ground, poor lighting, and even water on the floor. Modifying their homes to include bright lighting, heating, non-slip tiles and rugs, and handrails on stairs and in the bathroom is essential to keeping this group safe. This group are also at risk of fraud and violence. The group is seen as easy prey and is more likely to be taken advantage of. Knowing their rights and having people around them to alert them about scams is essential.

Employment for anyone can give feelings of self-worth and promote self-esteem. As the aged move into retirement they may reduce their working hours. As advancements in technology may make some of the aged unemployable, this group needs to have supportive workplaces that recognise the Equal Employment Opportunity Act that will continue to train staff.

Maintaining an adequate standard of living can be difficult for this group. For many the Age Pension is their only means of support. This means that a large proportion of this group have an inadequate standard of living. When an individual has a lower standard of living, an individual's sense of identity can be affected. Feelings of uselessness, due to reduced mobility and the inability to complete small tasks, may increase the need to seek a carer. The reliance on someone else and having to fit into someone else's timetable to get the support needed can impact on how a person sees himself or herself.

Access to services is also an issue of concern for the aged and includes **types of services** and **factors affecting access to services**.

Types of services: Many services are available to this group; however, there are many factors that make accessing these services difficult. Types of services the aged *require access to* may include:

Type of service	Examples
Financial support	Compulsory superannuation payments. The Department of Human services supports the War Widows Pension; Rent assistance, Pharmaceutical allowance, Pensioner concession care and Health Care Card.
Transport	Seniors card access to cheaper OPAL cards for public transport use. The NSW Community transport program, Dial and Angel – support with travel to and from appointments, taxi services, and many local clubs, such as an RSL club, will have community buses to take clients to and from home.

Accommodation and housing	There are many housing services. The types of housing and accommodation for this group include: individual housing, support from Commonwealth Home Support program; remain in home; Veterans Home Care; retirement villages; aged care nursing homes; and palliative care.
Health care	Telecross – run by Red Cross Australia, Meals on Wheels, day therapy centres, local GP and hospitals.
Counselling	Carers NSW provides counselling for aged people who are caring for loved ones; beyondblue and Lifeline.
Education	Broadband for seniors – aged 50+ years free access to computers, internet and basic training. Seniors information services, Council on the Ageing (COTA) peer educators program.
Employment	Lions Club volunteers, Oldworker.com.au, Care Career.
Legal aid	The Aged Rights Service (TARS) – My Aged Care, Aged Care Advocacy Program, Aged Care Complaints and Resolution.

Factors affecting access to services can be remembered by the acronym CAR. Characteristics of individuals within the group; e.g. first language spoken, culture, socioeconomic status, type of disability, age, gender, level of education (Lights. Camera. STAGE); aspects of the service, e.g. location, opening hours, confidentiality, staffing (LOCS); and resources, e.g. knowledge, energy, money, time (KEMT).

The individual characteristics of an aged person may influence their access to services. The age of a person is the defining characteristic that places them in this group. When a person reaches a certain age, more resources and more services become available. This is to ensure equity for this group.

Gender: Women on average live longer; male life expectancy is 80 years compared to the female life expectancy of 84 years. This may mean that women are worse off than males. They have had fewer opportunities to build up their superannuation, and may have fewer informal support networks to care for them; therefore, they need more services available later in life. This will influence an individual's socioeconomic status. The lower an individual's socioeconomic status, the more it limits the services available. If an aged person has a disability, or a disability occurs because of a person's age, it will influence their access to services. The ability to move to services, communicate with services, and see or hear when approaching services is hindered by a disability, as well as by the ageing process.

The level of education a person has will influence this group's superannuation funds. When a person is educated they are more likely to have gainful employment, increasing the opportunity for superannuation to accumulate. Unfortunately for the current aged and many baby boomers, because the Superannuation Act was only introduced in 1992, the superannuation they have is not enough to live off.

The culture and first language spoken of the members of this group will influence access to services. Many aged people came to Australia from Europe, fleeing war-torn countries. Language difficulties and cultural barriers may make a person fearful of government agencies, therefore limiting their access.

Aspects of the service will dictate whether a person can access it. Despite a service being available for use, if a service's opening hours are not suitable for when the individual needs it, the service will not be accessed. Generally, if this group is not working or they are phasing into their retirement, they have access to all services during their opening hours. However, if they are carers, being able to physically access the service may be an issue as they cannot leave their dependants. Caring for a highly dependent partner or grandchildren may make it physically impossible to use the service.

- Confidentiality: The confidentiality of a service may impact on the access to the service for the aged. Giving personal and private information may make an aged person wary of using the service – especially online services, as this group may not understand the security measures provided by the service. Therefore, this group may not use online banking or online shopping as they feel their details may be exposed.
- The location of some services may make it impractical or impossible for the aged to access. For the aged living in rural areas or where services are not located, accessing them will become an issue. With the government policy 'Living longer, living better', many aged services are now coming to the home of the aged person, enabling them to 'age in place' or 'age in their home'. The aged may need a taxi service to access some services, which may be costly.
- Staffing: For some aged people, wherever the setting, having to rely on strangers for personal daily help may be awkward and uncomfortable. For some this may mean refusal of all help, increasing the risks of major health issues. In order to access the 'Home Care Packages' under the 'Living longer, living better' policy, an Aged Care Assessment Team (ACAT) assesses the capabilities and level of independence an individual has. This requires the individual to answers very specific and personal questions. If the team is not sensitive to each person's needs, they may not get an accurate picture of the individual and may not assess their needs correctly. Depending on the individual circumstances, the aged individual may have suffered a stroke or may be impaired by medication, therefore staffing at services not specifically targeting the aged but accessed by the aged must be understanding of communication problems or sight/hearing difficulties. They must vary their support accordingly.

A lack of resources is another factor affecting access to services. Time is a resource that this group may be perceived to have a lot of; this may be due to the perception that all aged have stopped working. Members of this group still may be phasing their retirement or volunteering, thus limiting the time they have. As their bodies deteriorate, this group will need more time to communicate their needs and thoughts – thus they also need the human resource of patience. Eyesight may be poor thus this group may lose their ability to drive, and as mobility may also be an issue, this group will need more time to get to a service. These mobility issues may also limit the energy they have. Higher levels of fatigue are a characteristic of this group. This group may suffer from bone degeneration and the effects of lifestyle diseases, all of which can influence energy levels.

The government recognises that this group may have a low socioeconomic status and low resources of <u>money</u>. This group will use their savings from their superannuation scheme to live off, which may be limited and have to be subsidised by the age pension. To ensure this resource is used sustainability this group is supported by subsided gas and electricity bills, health care cards for cheaper medicine and cheaper health care, cheaper transport, movies and entry into attractions. <u>Knowledge</u> of the support services available will limit the use of them for the aged. The Council on the Ageing (COTA) provides peer educators, who are trained 65+ year olds who can communicate on the same level, with knowledge that is very specific to this stage of life.

Sample examination questions: Short answer

13 **Compare how available services within the community are for TWO groups you have studied**. (8 marks)

Youth can be defined as any person between 15 and 24 years old. The opening hours of the service may be an aspect that affects the group's access to a service, as they are likely to be studying full-time or involved in some pattern of work. The youth's advanced technology skills will assist them in accessing services online (such as eheadspace online support) and hotlines which are available 24 hours a day, e.g. KHL (Kids Helpline). This contrasts with the aged (those 65+ years), who are perceived to have an abundance of free time, as they are more likely to be undertaking phased retirement or are perhaps unemployed. However, unlike youth, the aged are less competent with technology and more likely to access the service in person. Both groups are likely to be carers (for the aged, their partners; for youth, younger siblings) and this will restrict their ability to access services with short opening hours.

Confidentiality will be an aspect of the service that may prevent access for both groups. Youth are likely to seek services for assistance with personal issues (i.e., mental health or sexual health); if they know the service is confidential it will encourage youth to share their problems with a counsellor or access websites like beyondblue. Similarly, the aged may be wary of sharing personal information. As this group is already very vulnerable to scams or may be perceived as naïve due to decreasing functioning of their senses and deteriorating mental capacity, they are less likely to share personal details online, e.g. online banking or through eBay, as they may feel as though their details are too exposed.

The location of a service will affect the accessibility as both groups are likely to be dependent on others for transport, and this may prove to be complicated if the distance is inconvenient. The aged have greater access to transport services, e.g. Commonwealth Home Support program, and are more likely to have the funds to pay for transport; however, both groups are eligible for transport cards.

For both the aged and youth, staffing of a service will be a factor that affects accessibility. Staff for both groups must focus on not being condescending or patronising. The staff offered to the aged is more likely to be intrusive as they may be assisting with personal tasks such as the Aged Care Assessment Team (ACAT) team, which assesses the skills and capabilities of aged persons prior to entering into a nursing home. For both groups, staff must be empathetic and attentive, as failure to do so may discourage the group from seeking further help.

Creating positive social environments

Students learn about:	Students learn to:
creating positive social environments *addressing the groups' issues of concern* • government policy and legislation • organisations within the community that support the group • equity issues	• examine government policy and legislation to determine its role in ensuring equity for each group • critically analyse the extent to which organisations within the community assist in satisfying the needs of each group • investigate a current inequity issue faced by each group and propose strategies to address the issue

Revision summary

When trying to change community attitudes and create a positive social environment it is important to eliminate issues that create inequity. By eliminating the group's issues of concern by satisfying specific needs and eliminating factors affecting access to services, the group will become equal in society. How do we eliminate the group's issues of concerns? Create government policy and legislation, provide organisations within the community and propose strategies to address equity issues.

Government policy plays an important role in ensuring equity for the aged. 'Living longer, living better' policy, Commonwealth Home Support program (formally HACC), the NSW Ageing Strategy, The *Aged Care Act, 1997*, the Superannuation Scheme, Anti-discrimination and Equal Employment Opportunity, Age Pension, *Veterans' Entitlements Act 1986 (Cwlth)* and the Pension Bonus scheme are all examples of policies and legislation that aim to align this group with the rest of society in terms of their living arrangements and their access to financial support.

Australia has many **organisations** designed to meet the needs of this group. Each organisation targets different aspects of this group, some meeting their day-to-day needs, others aiming to promote the overall feelings of satisfaction relating to wellbeing. This is turn can create equity for this group. Some organisations within the community that support the aged are the Australian Red Cross, COTA, The Salvation Army, Meals on Wheels, St Vincent de Paul, Community Transport organisation, Palliative Care Australia and Alzheimer's Australia.

Equity issues for this group surround the deterioration of their bodies. When the body deteriorates, an individual becomes vulnerable. Discrimination is an equity issue faced by this group. This could be in the workplace or when having to retake driving tests due to age. This group's security and safety is an equity issue, as they are vulnerable to the predatory behaviour of people who take advantage of this group. Equity issues may involve the construction of new buildings, confusing shapes in architecture, glass doors, heavy doors, revolving doors, faster moving escalators, poor colour contrasts, disorientating designs, dark underground parking and unnecessary noise. Any of these can make accessing services and navigating places difficult, leading to a lack of confidence. _Strategies to address the issue_ could be developed to ensure fairness and a sense of justice.

Sample examination questions: Short answer

14 **Explain how government policies and regulations have been developed to ensure equity for ONE of the groups listed below:** (8 marks)

- Aged
- Culturally and Linguistically Diverse communities
- Aboriginal and Torres Strait Islander peoples
- Rural and remote families
- Gay, Lesbian, Bisexual, Transgender and Intersex communities
- Sole parents
- Youth

(Adapted from BOS, 2012)

NB: You can insert any of the category B groups studied and answer the same questions accordingly.

Group: Aged

The aged are those who are more than 65 years old. As a minority group within society, the aged experience many inequities, and therefore government policy and legislation such as The 'Living longer, living better' policy supported by the Commonwealth Home Support program, the _Aged Care Act 1997_ and the superannuation scheme have been introduced to counteract it.

The superannuation scheme is another government policy that aims to provide equity (not necessarily for the current aged, but those future generations of aged people) by providing them with savings, which have accumulated from their working wage over time. This provides the aged with equity, as they will be able to spend their own money to maintain their own lifestyle, which is not offered by the Age Pension. This money also has tax benefits. Unfortunately, the superannuation scheme is not equitable for women, making them at risk of being at a lower socioeconomic status when they retire compared to men. This is because allowances have not been made for the time off work that women take when having children. The costs of living do not decrease for women as they get older and therefore they are at a big disadvantage in their retirement.

The Aged Care Act ensures equity for the aged by guaranteeing that the place of living that they have to enter – due to the deterioration of their body or mind as a result of ageing – reaches a high standard of quality care. This does provide equity for all. Although this law creates a high standard, due to the lack of aged care workers, specifically nurses, aged care facilities may be understaffed and not meeting the standard set out by the law.

The aged are often indirectly discriminated against within the workplace because employers are reluctant to hire this group as they are considered expensive (due to original training levels), coupled with the knowledge they will also have to retrain them in current practices. The implementation of the Equal Employment Opportunity Act attempts to reduce this, as it makes it against the law to discriminate on the basis of age, gender, race, marital status, disability or pregnancy.

15 **Propose strategies that can be implemented to address a current inequity issue faced by ONE of the groups listed below:** (6 marks)

- Aged
- Culturally and Linguistically Diverse communities
- Aboriginal and Torres Strait Islander peoples
- Rural and remote families
- Gay, Lesbian, Bisexual, Transgender and Intersex communities
- Sole parents
- Youth

(Adapted from BOSTES, 2014).

Group: Aged

For the aged (those 65 or more years of age) the most prominent inequity issue is the shortage of aged care workers, resulting in a low quality of care for those in aged care facilities. Due to the stigma around the aged, few people are seeking employment in the industry. A strategy to combat this is by educating younger generations to appreciate and respect the aged, such as the COTA-implemented Grandparents Day – inviting the aged into local primary schools so that young people experience first-hand their stories, see their skills and just spend time with them in a one-on-one capacity.

This will change the perception of how young people see the aged, thus it may encourage an increase in aged care workers as they will want to care for the group, not just because there are positions available.

Another strategy is the increase of wages, benefits, and training to make the job seem more desirable. Increasing desirability for a job will increase the numbers applying for the job. With an increase in competition to gain employment, only the best will gain employment – increasing the quality of care provided for the aged in residential care. Another strategy could be partnerships developed between nursing homes and universities, TAFEs and private colleges.

Guaranteed employment in places where students have done their training or workplaces which familiarise employees with policies and procedures prior to actually becoming employed ensure that transition into employment is smooth, thereby reducing the risks of leaving the profession after a few months of employment. This will ensure quality workers stay within aged care and will provide better trained quality workers, thus increasing the quality of care. The government could also adopt a strategy similar to the Dutch government, who offer free rent housing in exchange for the care of and interaction with the aged residents.

Positive influences on community attitudes

Students learn about:	Students learn to:

positive influences on community attitudes
• contributions the group makes within the community
• advocacy (speaking up for the group's needs and concerns)
  – raising awareness within the community
  – educating the community
  – promoting the rights of the group
	• explore ONE example of what each group has done to try to improve community attitudes, and assess the impact this has had on the wellbeing of the group
	• outline how community organisations advocate for each group and describe the positive influence it can have on community attitudes

Revision summary

The group has made and continues to make contributions to the community. **Recognising the contributions** that this group has directly made to the community around them will influence attitudes towards the group. This group has a vast age range; 65 years to the end of their average life expectancy can be 15 to 18 years, with many living beyond that. Ageing happens at different rates, therefore an individual's ability to contribute is dependent upon their individual circumstances.

With age comes experience, knowledge, wisdom and tradition. Without the aged it would be difficult to teach children about tradition. The aged are role models; they model hard work, teach skills and have knowledge from their vast experiences. They are a very important part of the family structure.

With lives being so busy, the aged have become an important part of the community too. They provide childcare for their grandchildren. While this is important to the family unit, it also supports the community and allows skilled women to return to the workforce. This increases the quality of goods and services that they support. Within the family unit, grandparents as carers are a trustworthy and cost-effective method of childcare.

Many of the aged have experienced times of war. This selflessness and love for their country has allowed democracy, and their participation has supported freedom within Australia.

The Australian community has also benefitted from the precision and skill this group has acquired. The infrastructure of roads, bridges, building, rail networks, and schemes such as the hydroelectric scheme ensures the quality of life that we live today. The speed at which goods and services can be moved around is the result of communication networks and travel networks built by this generation for the many generations that will follow.

COTA is a community organisation that endorses national Grandparents Day. This day has been introduced to show appreciation for the contribution that the aged makes to the community, with the aim to also improve community attitudes towards this group. This has influenced the wellbeing of the group.

Advocacy is about speaking up for the group's needs and concerns. Despite this group contributing to the community in many ways, they are vulnerable. As they age further, their ability to speak up for themselves and remain independent becomes difficult. This group becomes vulnerable because they are questioned – questioned about their ability, their skills and their memories. When this group starts to lose independence because of the deterioration of their bodies, they may be moved to aged care services, which are unfamiliar. This group may have lost their confidence and their self-esteem, and they may fear retribution if they do speak up. They may seek advocacy due to medical and health issues, like dementia or Alzheimer's disease, or they may have become isolated from family and friends and are unable to participate in the decisions affecting their lives.

Community organisations take on the role of advocating. COTA raises awareness for this group by endorsing Grandparents Day and the World Elder Abuse Awareness Day. On these days and through their work, they aim to educate the community by providing accurate, reliable and current information to the community. They have formed partnerships with legal aid to ensure the group is empowered with the knowledge to ensure their rights are met when they may have lost independence. 'Peer educator roles' are established through COTA, which meets the aged right to participation. Peers educating peers assists older people to receive information about legislative changes, community changes and home care packages.

Sample examination questions: Short answer

16 **Outline how community attitudes towards ONE group have been positively influenced by the community organisations who advocate for them. Choose from the list below.** (8 marks)

- Aged
- Culturally and Linguistically Diverse communities
- Aboriginal and Torres Strait Islander peoples
- Rural and remote families
- Gay, Lesbian, Bisexual, Transgender and Intersex communities
- Sole parents
- Youth

Group: Aged

The aged (those aged 65+ years) are a minority group within the community who are vulnerable and seek community organisations to speak up on their behalf. The Council on the Ageing (COTA) aims to raise awareness of this group through the endorsement of days in local schools like Grandparents Day. This day is aimed at educating the community from the younger generation up. This means that this group is more likely to experience support if younger people see their worth. By participating in days such as this, sharing stories and teaching young children new skills, the aged are meeting their right of participation. COTA has changed community attitudes towards this group, as attitudes can be formed from a very young age. Attitudes that may be formed from the media may be changed through seeing the skills of the aged and communicating on a one on one basis.

Alzheimer's Australia is a community organisation that creates awareness of the illnesses Alzheimer's disease and dementia, which are common brain diseases associated with ageing. Through campaigns like Dementia Awareness Month and World Alzheimer's Day, the greater population can be educated on the needs and early symptoms of sufferers. This will create early detection and access to medication to reduce some symptoms, increasing this group's rights to protection. This understanding and education about these diseases, which are so common, may allow people to rethink their attitudes related to someone who is speaking slowly or who may seem confused. This education may create empathy and support for this group.

Chapter 3

Parenting and Caring

Parenting and Caring is one of three compulsory modules in the HSC course and should occupy approximately 25 per cent of course time (BOS, 2013, p. 26).

Studying this core module will provide students with the recognition that becoming a parent can happen in more than just the traditional way. Biological and social parents and carers co-exist in society, and for social parents there are many impacts of change. Parents and carers will all have the same or similar role to play in dependants' lives to optimise the wellbeing of the dependant.

Caring is a large component of this core; whether an individual is a parent or carer, they will still face many similar experiences and circumstances, such as preparation, factors affecting the role they play and the support to which they have access. Students will gain the knowledge or recognition that parents and carers must fulfil multiple roles, and they will gain the skills to propose strategies to meet these roles. They will also gain skills to recognise support in the local community, its role in supporting parents and carers, and how community support may influence the lives of the people who access it.

HSC core 3: Parenting and Caring

Types of parents and carers

Students learn about:	Students learn to:

becoming a parent or carer
types of parents and carers
• biological parents
• social parents
  – adoption
  – fostering
  – step-parenting
  – surrogacy
	• describe the different types of parents and carers
	• explore the impact of legal, social and technological change on social parents by considering changes in:
	  – legislation
	  – community beliefs and attitudes
	  – reproductive technology

Revision summary

A parent is considered to be biological if the child has their genetic make-up. In the contemporary world, this is no longer the only way to become a parent. Individuals may become a social parent, which may have legislation governing the role, community beliefs and attitudes and for surrogate social parents, reproductive technology is needed.

Adoption is when biological parents relinquish all rights to their child, passing these rights to the adoptive parents, who assume all parental rights and responsibilities.

When a child is adopted from another country (inter-country adoption) the process can be legally complicated. Abiding by Australian laws as well as the adopting country's laws can be confusing. Thus there are agencies to support this process. When a child physically looks different from their adoptive parents, the adoptive process is apparent to the community. This can have its own social impacts on the child and family.

When a child is fostered, it means they can no longer be with their biological parents for any number of reasons: parental mental health issues, illness such as cancer or incarceration, or the child may be at risk of domestic or sexual abuse. Foster parents are administered by Family and Community Services (FACS), which means FACS makes all the decisions regarding the child's care, schooling, medical, contact with other people coming into the family home, access to holidays and visitation with biological parents if possible. Living with foster parents can lead to questions surrounding the child's biological family, which can lead to frustration and emotional fear, especially if the circumstances in which the child was placed were traumatic.

An individual will become a step-parent when they form a relationship with another adult who has children from a previous relationship. Step-parents will have no legal rights over the child; this makes decision-making difficult for this parent. Unfortunately, the media presents step-parents with a negative stereotype. The attitude towards a step-parent may be influenced by the age of the children and the biological parents.

A surrogate is a woman who gives birth to a child on behalf of a couple who are either infertile or same sex. There are no specific laws supporting surrogacy, which make this type of social parenting difficult. Paying a surrogate is illegal in Australia, which has led many prospective parents to travel to other countries to seek a surrogate. This risks the exploitation of women, who can earn a large amount of money in a relatively short period. The surrogate relies on the use of reproductive technology to fall pregnant and because of this she will be deemed the mother of this child by the courts until a parentage order can be commissioned. This highly complex process is relatively expensive, time consuming and can be emotionally draining.

Sample examination questions: Multiple choice

1   **What types of social parents have day-to-day responsibilities for a child but no legal rights?**
    (A) Adoptive and foster
    (B) Foster and step-parent
    (C) Surrogate and adoptive
    (D) Step-parent and surrogate
    (BOS, 2012)

2   **In the case of surrogacy, the birth mother**
    (A) must be related to the family.
    (B) should not receive payment for the child.
    (C) has the same legal rights as adoptive parents.
    (D) can make day-to-day decisions regarding the child.
    (BOSTES, 2014)

3   **A foster parent is best described as a person who**
   (A) has legal rights for the child.
   (B) takes on the role of a temporary parent or carer of a child.
   (C) becomes pregnant and gives birth to a child for another person.
   (D) takes on the role of a parent as a result of a marriage or a de facto
       relationship.
   (BOS, 2013)

4   **Cathy lives in a de facto relationship with Chris who has two children.**
   What type of parent is Cathy in relation to Chris's children?
   (A) Voluntary
   (B) Foster
   (C) Step
   (D) Surrogate
   (BOSTES, 2014)

Sample examination questions: Short answer

1   **The table below shows adoptions in Australia over the last 20 years.**

Approximate number of adoptions in Australia

	1991–1995	1996–2000	2001–2005	2006–2010
Children adopted from within Australia	3191	1730	969	850
Children adopted from overseas	1404	1333	1665	1587
Total adoptions in Australia	4595	3063	2634	2437

From the table, give ONE reason for the change in adoption data over
the 20-year period. (3 marks) (BOS, 2012)

Over the past 20 years we can see that adoption numbers have dramatically
decreased, from 4595 down to 2437. One reason for the change in Australian
adoption data over the 20-year period is the increase in birth technologies
available. People have many more options available to them if they cannot have
children naturally than they did 20 years ago. With better technology and better
success rates, families are not relying on adoption to start their family if they are
having reproductive issues.

2   **Discuss the legal and social implications of surrogacy.** (6 marks) (BOS,
   2013)

Surrogacy is the arrangement between a woman and a couple. The intention is
that the woman will have a baby for the couple and the couple will raise and care
for the child.

LEGAL: There are many positives and negatives relating to surrogacy. The laws
surrounding surrogacy differ from state to state. One law is common,
'commercial' surrogacy is illegal. This means that women who are surrogates are

not paid (other than medical costs provided) in Australia, resulting in a limited number of women being available for infertile or same sex couples. In cases where these couples cannot find a surrogate within Australia, they may go to countries such as India or the USA, where commercial surrogacy is legal. This may cause international surrogates to be exploited, especially in developing countries around the world.

Another negative of the laws, or lack of laws, surrounding surrogacy is that the woman who delivers the baby (the surrogate) is deemed the biological parent and has all rights over the child, despite any contracts or previous arrangements. This may lead to the intended couple walking away without the child after birth.

SOCIAL: Social surrogacy arrangements can include up to five different adults: the surrogate, the two intended parents and perhaps another egg donor and sperm donor. This may be positive as the child may have five supportive people in their life. This may also be a negative as too many people may try to claim custody of the child, and with the lack of supportive laws in Australia, the emotional impact on a child may be devastating.

Surrogacy, if it is successful for the intended couple, is a positive, as this couple may have been through years and years of fertility treatment, which is expensive and very emotionally draining. When they finally have their child, they may be living in shock and unable to believe it is real for a period of time, but be completely ecstatic that they finally have a family!

Becoming a parent or carer

Students learn about:	Students learn to:

becoming a parent or carer
 • carers
   – primary
   – formal and informal
	• examine current research data on primary carers to determine the:
	   – significance of age and gender
	   – reasons for carers taking on the role, e.g. emotional obligation, alternative care too costly

Revision summary

A carer is someone who takes on the role of fulfilling and meeting the needs of someone else. They may need to fulfil all their needs, or only some, depending on the skills and capabilities of the dependant.

Primary carers are those carers who provide the majority of informal assistance – they are usually related in some way to the dependant and for this reason they often provide care because they feel it is their family responsibility, and they have emotional obligations to the dependant. The carer may feel like there is not another family member who can provide the same level of care, or they may not have any other alternatives as formal care may be too costly. There may even be mistrust from previous experiences with formal care. Formal carers are paid carers or volunteers who work in structured organisations. These carers choose to take on this role for various reasons, including career development, e.g. volunteering in aged care to become a nurse, or as a career. As a trained professional formal carer, care is a means to access economic resources to ensure their needs are met. Formal carers will also usually care because they enjoy helping others and their personality lends itself to nurturing and fulfilling other people's needs.

Current research and statistics show that carers can be any age, e.g. young people caring for a sick parent, a parent with mental health issues or their main caregiver grandparent. Carers can also be aged, caring for their elderly partner or family. However, they are mostly between the ages of 35 and 64 years. This may be linked to the ageing population and younger family members having to support their ageing parents. Carers are most often women, with over half of all carers in Australia (primary, informal and formal) being women (ABS, 2012).

Sample examination questions: Multiple choice

5   **Why does the government provide financial assistance to carers?**
(A) To provide educational opportunities for the carers
(B) To provide educational opportunities for those in care
(C) To provide for carers who are often unable to participate in the workforce
(D) To provide for those in care who are often unable to participate in the workforce
(BOS, 2012)

6   Which of the following are ALL examples of paid carers?
(A) Nurses, childcare workers, nannies
(B) Respite carers, biological parents, nurses
(C) Step-parents, surrogate parents, health care workers
(D) Grandparents, childcare workers, after school carers
(BOS, 2012)

7   Which of the following is an example of an unpaid carer in an
     unplanned circumstance?
(A) A community health nurse visiting a new mother
(B) A wife caring for her husband following an accident
(C) A nurse attending to individuals in the emergency ward of a hospital
(D) A staff member providing programs for children in a classroom
(BOS, 2013)

Sample examination questions: Short answer

3   Trends show the following:
     1) Females are more likely to be carers
     *2) There is a large increase in the number of carers between the ages of
         35 years to 64 years.*
     Account for ONE of these trends. (2 marks)

Females are more likely to be carers, as it is a societal stereotype that females
are generally more caring and nurturing. When they become a parent they
acquire more skills to care, thus when they are take time off from working to care
for their children, they may also take on the caring role for their ageing parents or
grandparents.

The roles of parents and carers

Students learn about:	Students learn to:
becoming a parent or carer *the roles of parents and carers* • satisfying the specific needs of the dependant • building a positive relationship with the dependant • promoting the wellbeing of the dependant	• outline the roles of parents and carers and evaluate the significance of each role in various parenting and caring situations

Revision summary

Once an individual becomes a parent or carer, whether biologically, socially, as a primary carer or as a formal/informal carer, they have a set role to fulfil for the dependant in their care. All parents and carers must satisfy the **specific needs** of the dependant. This means that as a parent or carer, it is your job to ensure your child, or the person in your care, must have their security and safety needs, sense of identity, health, adequate standard of living, and employment. If the parent or carer cannot satisfy these needs, it is their role to ensure they have the tools to fulfil this need for themselves. In order to promote wellbeing or satisfy some needs (such as security and safety), parents and carers must build a **positive relationship with the dependant**. Building a positive relationship relies on building a bond based on honesty, trust and communication. To **promote the wellbeing of a dependant** and to allow them to feel a degree of satisfaction, parents and carers must ensure needs. The broad areas of Social, physical, emotional, cultural, economic and spiritual factors must be addressed and fulfilled in order for the dependant to achieve wellbeing. All three of these roles work in conjunction with each other and are interrelated; they are dependent upon each other for the dependant to achieve the satisfaction in their life associated with wellbeing.

Sample examination question: Short answer

4   A grandmother has had to take on the primary care of her three grandchildren, aged 8, 12 and 13, because their mother and father were involved in a fatal car accident. What is the significance of parenting and caring roles in this caring situation? (3 marks)

The grandmother through this critical time will have to satisfy the specific needs of her grandchildren. At this time, they may be feeling vulnerable and confused. Fulfilling their security and safety needs by moving into the children's home will ensure a familiar environment that supports their sense of identity needs and allows their education needs to be met by returning to a supportive school environment. Their adequate standard of living needs will also be met, at least to the same or similar standard as when they were living with their parents.

Because the carer is their grandmother, these children may have already had a positive relationship with her, which they can hopefully maintain. However, everyone deals with grief differently and relationships may be strained if new rules and limits are set. If needs are generally satisfied and relationships are positive, this will promote the wellbeing of the dependants. Economic factors relating to the wellbeing of dependants will be dictated by the socioeconomic status of the family before the accident, the grandmother's socioeconomic status and whether the grandmother can access employment.

Preparations for becoming a parent or carer

Students learn about:	Students learn to:
becoming a parent or carer *preparations for becoming a parent or carer* • changing health behaviours, e.g. nutrition, physical activity, social or spiritual connections • enhancing knowledge and skills, e.g. education, information, training • modifying the physical environment e.g. housing, amenities, equipment • organising finances, e.g. budgeting, saving, support payments	• examine a range of parenting and caring situations and assess the impact preparations can have on the wellbeing of the dependant

Revision summary

When an individual becomes a parent or carer, it may come about through many different circumstances. Social parents may not have the opportunity to prepare for the birth of a child in nine months. Those adopting from overseas may receive a phone call and at short notice they will meet their new child. Crisis foster carers may receive a phone call in the middle of the night and start caring for a child immediately. When a family member is involved in an accident or is diagnosed with an acute illness, a carer is needed immediately. Situations like this can increase the difficulty of preparing.

Changing health behaviours. Health is holistic and encompasses physical, social, emotional, spiritual and cultural health. Changing health behaviours may mean that expectant mothers modify their diets, while carers need to increase their intake to ensure they have the energy to care for themselves and others. For a carer having to look after the elderly or physically disabled they may have to learn lifting techniques. To cope with the new situation, parents and carers will need a support structure in place, and they may have to make new social or spiritual connections

Enhancing knowledge and skills, e.g. education, information, training. In order to cope with situations that are different or new, a new parent or carer can increase their understanding by going to courses, reading books, blogs, and information booklets, and talking to experts. Seeking out support groups will enhance the knowledge of parents and carers to find out new strategies that have worked in similar situations. Attending a training course, such as an antenatal class, will give hands-on skills and teach expectant parents some skills so that they may cope in new circumstances.

Modifying the physical environment e.g. housing, amenities, equipment. Changing the environment by modifying the house, moving, buying new equipment and adding amenities to meet the needs of a dependant is important when preparing for a new parenting/caring situation. In situations where the mobility of the dependant becomes an issue, widening doorways to suit wheelchairs or walkers, installing ramps and hand rails, and increasing the lighting to reduce risks of falls are all steps new carers can implement to fulfil duty of care responsibilities. Equipment may also need to be purchased or hired to support bathing and toileting. For new parents, preparing a nursery will involve safe sleeping solutions such as a cot or bassinet, temperature control to reduce the risk of SIDs and baby proofing the house.

Organising finances, e.g. budgeting, saving, support payments. Ensuring there are enough economic resources to cover needs is essential to organise finances. Creating a clear budget, recognising any money coming into the situation and what will need to be bought or paid for will help parents and carers preparing for their circumstances. Prior savings can be used for initial outlay of purchases, however, depending on the situation, savings may need to be used sparingly to enable more time away from work, especially if the dependant will need long-term care. The government will support parents and carers, however, new parents and carers will need to apply to Centrelink and provide supporting documents to receive these payments.

Sample examination question: Multiple choice

8   **Jenny and Ian have recently found out they are expecting triplets. Jenny and Ian can best prepare their physical environment in this situation by:**
(A) attending a support group.
(B) making adjustments to their home.
(C) organising private health insurance.
(D) contacting Centrelink to seek assistance.
(Adapted from BOSTES, 2014)

Sample examination questions: Short answer

5   **Explain how organising finances can affect preparations for becoming a parent or carer.** (5 marks) (Adapted from BOSTES, 2014)

Organising finances is the recognition of money available and allocating it to meet different needs, e.g. purchasing equipment, paying bills, organising household modifications or paying for medical expenses. When there is a surplus of money, usually through income, identifying needs and preparing for them is made easier.

For those with limited money, or for those in a situation that was unplanned, preparations may be rushed, resulting in stress. When a parenting or caring situation arises, creating a clear budget is essential. A budget will create a clear plan of what income/money is available and what must be used for essential items. For example, when a new baby arrives, time off can be planned for. Accessing paid maternity leave (if available) will enable a new mother to see how much money is coming into the household so she can compare her expenses and decide how long she can afford to be off work for.

When a situation is planned for, parents and carers are more likely to have saved for it. They may have put aside money each week to prepare for large outlays of money such as fitting out a nursery or buying a pram. However, when unexpected situations occur, like a mother who is a casual worker developing cancer and having to leave the workplace, her ability to have saved may be limited. In this situation, creating a new budget and accessing support payments maybe be essential to meeting adequate standard of living needs.

Support payments made through the government (Centrelink) or through worker's compensation will enable the parent or carer to manage the situation. These limited payments will cover essentials, however they will not cover everything, and parents and carers will have to rely on their budgets and savings.

6   Describe the impact that modifying the physical environment has on physical and emotional factors of wellbeing. (3 marks)

Changing the environment when a dependant ages, becomes ill or is injured or when a new dependant is born is essential to limiting physical factors and emotional factors on wellbeing. If the physical environment is not changed when preparing to become a carer, the dependant may experience ill-being.

When modifying the physical environment when preparing to become a carer for an aged person, dangerous areas such as stairs, slippery tiles and dark areas will all need to be modified. Installing ramps, providing non-slip mats and tiles, widening doorways and increasing lighting will ensure the safety of the dependant. These physical factors will ensure safety, allowing free movement around their new living area and enhancing the dependants' overall wellbeing.

By eliminating the physical factors influencing wellbeing, emotional factors such as stress and reduced confidence will also be reduced. When dependants' capabilities are not hindered by trip hazards and safety concerns, their levels of carefree living, independence and peace of mind increase, as do their self-esteem and confidence, influencing their overall wellbeing. Modifying the physical environment will enhance not only their overall wellbeing but also their quality of life.

Characteristics of the dependant

Students learn about:	Students learn to:
factors affecting the roles of parents and carers *characteristics of the dependant* • age • skills/capabilities • special needs, e.g. illness, disability	• describe how the characteristics of the dependant can affect the roles of the parent or carer

Revision summary

The characteristics of the dependant will affect the roles of parents and carers. The **age** of a dependant will influence the roles of the parents and carers. Parents and carers take on the roles of satisfying the dependant's specific needs, building positive relationships and promoting wellbeing. When a dependant is young, such as an infant or toddler, parents and carers take responsibility to fulfil each role. Parents will spend large amounts of time satisfying their specific needs, such as health and adequate standard of living – food, clothing and shelter – as dependants do not have the skills or capabilities to satisfy them at all. As a child gets older, they may be able to start to develop some independence; they may fulfil some health needs themselves, for example, tasks relating to hygiene and exercise. At this time, parents may spend more time on promoting wellbeing by encouraging positive relationships with grandparents and other family members, which will encourage the passing down of cultural traditions. The older the dependant, the greater need for the parent/carer to support the development of independence and a sense of identity. As an older dependant may push boundaries and limits, it is important that building a positive relationship remains a focus.

Acquiring skills and capabilities is the learning of tasks that will enable the dependant to fulfil some of their own needs and promote their own wellbeing. When a dependant lacks skills and capabilities, parents and carers will have to satisfy all needs, promote wellbeing and work on maintaining open lines of communication to build a positive relationship. For a dependant who is high functioning, they can work together with their parents or carers to ensure all needs are met; they may have built resiliency to promote their own wellbeing, and they may have the skills and capabilities to help support less able family members, such as a young sibling, in tasks such as preparing a simple breakfast.

When a dependant has **special needs**, has an illness or injury, age will not define the skills and capabilities that they will have acquired. Depending on the special need, a dependant (low functioning) may fully rely on the parent or carer to promote their wellbeing, including the fulfilment of physical factors such as toileting and bathing. When a dependant relies on a parent/carer, building a positive relationship may be difficult. Dependants can become angry and frustrated at the situation, leading to conflict. For those with a special need who have some skills and capabilities, they may just need support in daily tasks, or be given the opportunity to meet others to promote their social aspects of wellbeing.

Sample examination questions: Short answer

7   In what ways can building a positive relationship be influenced by the age of the dependant? (3 marks) (Adapted from BOS, 2013)

A positive relationship can be built from birth. When a parent holds, talks to, makes eye contact and even breastfeeds, a bond and closeness is established. As a child grows and is a toddler, positive relationships continue to build by spending time, communicating clearly and creating a toddler 'proof' or safe environment where the child can explore and grow and feel safe.

When a dependant reaches their teen years, building a positive relationship may be difficult, especially if there hasn't been a relationship since birth, for example with step-parents or foster carers. Building trust, setting clear limits, and having negotiated and clear guidelines for discipline will help support this.

If a dependant is older, for example an ageing parent, building a positive relationship will rely on communication and the dependant's ability to maintain their own independence and sense of identity.

8   Describe how the characteristics of the dependant may affect a carer's role. (4 marks)

Characteristics of the dependant refer to the dependant's age, skills and capabilities, and special needs. The age of the dependant affects the carer's role. The younger the dependant, the less independent they are, and they may need assistance with simple daily tasks such as showering or dressing themselves as they lack experience. This affects the carers, as it will take more time to fulfil their role of meeting specific needs because the dependant is unable to. The skills and capabilities of the dependant refer to the skills that are acquired through experiences, such as being taught to cook. A dependant with more skills and capabilities will be able to fulfil many of their own needs, thus affecting the carer's role.

More time will be spent on building and establishing a positive relationship when a dependant has a special need such as cystic fibrosis, which may affect their quality of life. A carer seeks to promote the wellbeing of the dependant by meeting their health needs and enabling a sense of identity, thus emotional factors will satisfy wellbeing.

Influences on parents and carers: Personal

Students learn about:	Students learn to:

factors affecting the roles of parents and carers
influences on parents and carers
• personal
   – culture, customs and tradition
   – religion/spirituality
   – education
   – previous experience
   – own upbringing
   – multiple commitments, work, study, sport, family
   – socioeconomic status
   – special needs, e.g. illness/disability
	• examine each influence to determine its effect on parenting and caring
	• propose strategies to assist parents and carers to manage their multiple commitments

Revision summary

When an individual becomes a parent or carer, they bring in their own unique set of ideas, dictated by their values and standards. The values and standards a parent/carer has and sets will be influenced by certain factors in their life. These will dictate how they parent, what rules are established, how needs are met, the style of parenting they use and the relationship they have with their child.

Culture, religion and spirituality will influence how a parent/carer spends their time. It will influence the customs and traditions passed down to younger generations, the foods they eat, clothes they wear and who they spend their time with. Having a lifestyle influenced by a culture or religion will provide parents or carers with a set of expectations that will guide their choices.

The education levels of a parent/carer may determine their values towards education, which in turn will influence where a dependant goes to childcare, pre-school, and primary/high school. It may determine whether a child is encouraged to continue to further education or if they are support to leave school to gain an apprenticeship or traineeship.

When a parent or carer has a positive experience, they rely on that experience and may try to recreate the situation or allow that situation to guide future choices. For example, if a carer used a particular health care service, e.g. a physiotherapist, for the dependant and the quality of the service is high and the dependant forms a bond, the carer is more likely to use the service again. Using previous experiences to support future choices will help in the decision-making process, allowing confident, rational decisions to be made. The same will apply to negative experiences; parents and carers will change their course of action in similar situations.

The parents'/carers' own upbringing will influence how they parent or care. It can be said parenting/caring styles are cyclic and parents/carers follow similar routines to that of their parents or carers. This will occur in situations where they are happy with their own upbringing and supportive of the methods used on them. In instances where there is discontent with their experiences, parents and carers may make a conscious effort to change their dependant's future.

Socioeconomic status (SES) will influence the resources available for parents and carers. When parents or carers experience low socioeconomic status, choices and options are limited by money. This may mean these parents/carers rely on government support and health care covered by Medicare. When a family enjoys high socioeconomic status, dependants can experience close bonds with their parent/s through shared experiences or their relationships may suffer as parent/s may rely on carers as they are working long hours to maintain their status.

A special need will influence how an individual parents or cares, depending on who has the special need (parent, carer or dependant) and how much the special need affects daily functioning. When it is the parent or carer with the special need, such as a mental health issue, they may need their dependant to support them, as much as they provide support for their dependant. When the dependant has special needs, parents and carers will need to be aware of the daily affects the illness, disability or injury will have on their lives. This will affect how they fulfil their roles as parents and carers.

In today's society, many individuals are taking on more than one role; they are workers, parents, carers and volunteers, all while they are studying, pursuing leisure activities and following religion. Each of these roles comes with a set of demands. Meeting these many multiple role expectations will require strategies to be put in place to ensure the emotional stability of parents/carers and dependants. Managing resources, negotiating and sharing roles, utilising technology and using supportive workplace structures are some strategies to support parents and carers. (For more information on this, see Chapter 5.)

Sample examination questions: Multiple choice

9   **Which of the following strategies could best help parents manage their multiple roles?**
(A) Joining a social club
(B) Taking on a second job
(C) Refinancing their home loan
(D) Outsourcing household tasks
(BOS, 2013)

10   **Which combination of factors has the greatest personal influence on parenting and caring?**
(A) Age and nutrition
(B) Culture, customs and traditions and own upbringing
(C) Media stereotypes and special needs
(D) Gender and reproductive technology
(Adapted from BOS, 2013)

11   A mother uses information she has read on the internet on the benefits of using creative solutions in disciplining children to become a better mother. What has influenced the parenting approach of this mother?
(A) Media stereotypes
(B) Gender perceptions
(C) Previous experience
(D) Socioeconomic status
(Adapted from BOSTES, 2014)

Sample examination questions: Short answer

9   Outline strategies to assist parents and carers in managing their multiple commitments. (4 marks)

When parents have many demands to fulfil as a result of taking on many roles, they must implement strategies to enable the smooth running of the household. Strategies parents and carers could implement include:

Interchangeability of resources – this is useful when a parent in a leadership position at work is spending long hours there. They may swap the excess money they earn for someone else's time to clean the house.

A busy parent or carer may use technology to save time. Using a robotic vacuum cleaner instead of a hand held one will not only save time but also energy, as it requires effort to push the hand held around.

When a parent/carer is busy volunteering for their child's school they can use rosters and calendars to organise their time. The use of a roster will create a clear guide as to who completes what role. Having a visual roster will increase the likelihood of the jobs being completed.

A carer might access support like respite care if they need some time off. When a carer has to care, parent other dependants and perhaps work, they may need some time away, especially if they are the primary carer. Informal supports can also be used, for example if a working mother leaves work too late to pick up their child from school.

10   How will culture, customs and traditions influence caring for a grandparent? (3 marks)

Culture, customs and traditions will influence the care for a grandparent whether the carer shares the same culture, customs and traditions or if they differ. In formal support caring situations, for example when grandparents are cared for in a nursing home, their culture and traditions may not be recognised. There may be language barriers, foreign foods and differing traditions.

However, when caring for a grandparent in an informal setting, the grandparent has usually taught their children and grandchildren the customs and traditions of their culture. The impact of this on the grandparent's sense of identity needs will be enormous. They will feel a sense of pride and belonging if they hear familiar languages or they can witness a grandchild's involvement in a celebratory tradition such as Chinese New Year.

Influences on parents and carers: Social

Students learn about:	Students learn to:

factors affecting the roles of parents and carers: Influences *on parents and carers*
• social
  – community attitudes
  – gender expectations
  – media stereotypes
	• describe how social influences affect the roles of parents and carers
	• critically analyse expectations of males and females in parenting and caring roles in a changing society
	• explore one example of how a parent or carer may challenge social influences and assess the impact this can have on their wellbeing

Revision summary

Social influences on parents are the unsaid feelings and powers from society that sway parents and carers to act and fulfil their roles in a certain way.

Community attitudes: The community around you may influence how you parent. It may be led by an experienced leader, a media source or just a group of like-minded people. This may influence how to care, which foods to feed the dependant, whether to breast feed or bottle feed, whether to vaccinate or not, which clothing brands to use, whether to home school, when to return to work or even something as simple as what brand of washing powder to use. Many new mothers or carers may just follow their more experienced counterparts as they conform to those around them.

Gender expectations: Society created the roles that individuals are likely to take on based on their gender and previous stereotypes. Today we are seeing more people break away from stereotypes; however, some cultures and an individual's pervious experiences may lead people to remain in the traditional roles of males and females.

Media stereotypes: The media also has a hand in creating stereotypes; these may relate to gender, but will also relate to the role a parent should take on, how they take on that role and what products they need to take on that role. Parents and carers are bombarded with messages daily and hourly through access to smartphones and social media. Parents and carers may pick up unrealistic expectations and stereotypes, which may cause undue stress on the dependant and personal guilt when they cannot meet these expectations, or break away from the stereotypes, set by the media.

Sample examination questions: Short answer

11 Identify one example of how a carer may challenge social influences and outline the impact on their wellbeing. (3 marks)

A male can challenge the gender expectations of a paid carer. Becoming a male nurse, primary school teacher or childcare worker means that they are challenging society's views that females are the caring and nurturing gender. This may have a positive influence in his life as he may gain self-esteem and a sense of identity, knowing that he is caring and helping a sick patient (in the case of a male nurse). It may also make him feel socially isolated in the lunchroom or staffroom if he is the only male. He may feel judged, and his masculinity and sexuality may be questioned. These factors will influence his wellbeing both socially and emotionally.

12 Explain how social influences on parents and carers affect the roles of parents and carers. (8 marks)

Community attitudes refer to the social norms of society or the community. They influence parents and carers and the roles they undertake, and they have a major effect when trying to implement these roles. For example, a mother who decides to breastfeed her child until the age of four can be seriously affected and influenced by the attitudes of the community, as it is not the norm to breastfeed to this late age. The mother may find it hard to satisfy the health needs of her child as she may feel isolated or judged when breastfeeding her child in public. It may also affect her ability to build a positive relationship with her child, as she may not always be able to continue to bond with her child through breastfeeding as she may be with someone who disagrees with what she is doing.

Gender expectations are often cyclic within families and refer to the roles which both males and females take on in the parenting and caring setting. In today's society, we are seeing males taking more time off work to spend with their children. Women in many families are the breadwinner, so it makes more sense for them to return to the workforce and have their partner care for the children. Men typically get judged if they take on a caring role, such as a childcare worker, and may experience embarrassment or loss of pride. This affects the male carer's ability to build a positive relationship as they may feel as though they are being 'watched', especially if they become close with the children they are looking after.

Media stereotypes refer to the stereotypes created through TV, radio and social media. Often parents are exposed to TV shows that depict the perfect parents and household. This may affect their ability to promote their child's wellbeing as they create pressure situations, hoping the child will live up to this 'fake reality', and they try to display the perfect parenting style. If failure occurs, parents may feel guilt, and social isolation and mental health issues such as depression or anxiety. They may be unable to perform simple parenting tasks, thus affecting the role of satisfying specific needs. The relationship between parent and child or carer and child will also be strained, causing conflict. Emotional factors will influence the promotion of wellbeing.

Styles of parenting or caring

Students learn about:	Students learn to:
factors affecting the roles of parents and carers: *styles of parenting or caring* • authoritarian • democratic • permissive/indulgent • negligent	• explore each parenting or caring style and assess the impact it can have on the roles of parents and carers

Revision summary

The style of parenting or caring an individual adopts may be linked to their own previous experiences, the age of the dependant and perhaps their cultural expectations. The style of parenting or caring the individual adopts will influence how they *fulfil their roles* of a parent or carer (i.e. satisfy specific needs, build a positive relationship and promote wellbeing).

An **authoritarian parenting style** displays strict rules and limits. There is a clear expectation that dependants will follow the rules, and if they are broken, the consequences will be harsh. There may be a lot of experiences but limited freedom within those experiences to relax and have fun. Communication is clear, but the tone is firm, and there is no negotiation, but rather an intention that the dependant follows instruction. This style of parenting will aim to satisfy all needs. The parent may aim to build a positive relationship; however, young people may not respond to this style. When limits are pushed and young people try to establish independence, conflict and stress may occur, limiting *the promotion of wellbeing*.

A **democratic style** of parenting/caring relies on the lines of communication to be clear; equality in the decision-making process and discussion when negotiating limits and rules are key characteristics of this style. It is hoped that through the time spent with the dependant their behaviour will lift to parental/carer expectation; however, if it does not, the consequences are clear and related. The trust placed on the dependant to do the right thing encourages the *building of positive relationships*. Open, honest and trusting words used to describe the relationship develop when a democratic parenting style is used. This style of parenting will *satisfy all specific needs,* including a sense of identity, as these dependants are able to make their own mistakes, accept them and learn from them, encouraging independence.

A **permissive parenting/caring** style is a very lenient style of parenting/caring. There are very few demands placed on the child, and they are free to behave however they choose. Indulgent parenting/caring is characterised by parents/carers being highly involved in all aspects of the dependant's life, but few demands and limits are set. If limits are broken, responsibility is not taken and blame is placed elsewhere. This style of parenting/caring may be confusing for the child; however, the confusion is superseded by the lack of demand and freedom. It may be difficult to develop a *positive relationship* with this dependant as relationships rely on give and take, and this dependant has only experienced take.

Negligent parenting and caring is when the dependants' _needs are not satisfied_. This dependant may never experience the general feeling of _satisfaction relating to wellbeing,_ as they have had to strive to achieve it with little direction. In negligent parenting/caring cases, government agencies may remove the dependant from care and place them with a loving family who can satisfy their basic needs and aim to develop the positive relationship.

Sample examination questions: Multiple choice

12 Sam is 13 years old and has asked his parents if he can go to a party at his friend's house on Saturday night. Consider the following possible responses from Sam's parents in reply to this request. (BOS, 2012)

Response 1: _You will not be going_
Response 2: _I think we need to sit and discuss this together._
Response 3: _I don't mind, as long as you have finished your homework._
Response 4: _I don't care what you do._

Which of the responses listed above reflect authoritarian and negligent parenting styles?

	Parenting style	
	Authoritarian	Negligent
(A)	Response 1	Response 2
(B)	Response 1	Response 4
(C)	Response 2	Response 3
(D)	Response 2	Response 4

13 Holly is 15 years old, the eldest of three children and receives a large allowance. Holly's parents travel frequently and Holly is responsible for caring for her younger siblings. Which of the following best describes this style of parenting?
(A) Authoritarian
(B) Democratic
(C) Indulgent
(D) Negligent
(BOSTES, 2014)

Sample examination questions: Short answer

13 **Describe TWO styles of parenting or caring and examine the impact that each has on the roles of parents and carers.** (Adapted from BOSTES, 2014)

Authoritarian Parenting and Negligent Parenting.
An authoritarian parent is one who dictates over their dependant's life and exercises control in all decision-making and discipline. Depending on the living environment, the dependant and parent living in this type of parenting will positively or negatively impact on the satisfaction of their roles. For example, if a child or dependant and their parents are living in a war zone, this style of parenting may be essential for safety and security needs, promoting the physical factors of wellbeing. This will build a positive relationship because the dependant will understand that these strict rules are in place to ensure their life isn't in danger. However, if this style of parenting is in a safe environment it can negatively impact on their sense of identity, as the dependant will have little opportunity to express him or herself and explore the world around them. Emotional factors influencing wellbeing will be affected, as the dependant will be too afraid to make mistakes or take risks, causing anxiety. This can negatively affect the building of a positive relationship between parent and child as the child may feel resentful, restricted and controlled.

A negligent parent is one who does not nurture or protect a child. Their needs are rarely satisfied and the promotion of wellbeing comes down the child and their ability to satisfy their own needs. This style of parenting usually involves government support networks such as FACS intervention. This style of parenting will not satisfy their child's specific needs such as safety and security, sense of identity and sometimes their adequate standard of living; the neglectful nature will not nurture or protect a child/dependant. It will not promote the social or emotional factors of wellbeing as the child may not have attained sound morals and values passed down by a parent, therefore making it difficult to conform to society. Since the dependent may feel neglected and unwanted, it may cause lifelong impacts on emotional wellbeing. This style of parenting does not foster the building of positive relationships, as there will be no bond, connection or respect between dependant and parent.

Rights and responsibilities in parenting and caring

Students learn about:	Students learn to:

factors affecting the roles of parents and carers
rights and responsibilities in parenting and caring
• legal rights of parent, carers and dependants
• responsibilities of parents and carers
  – duty of care
  – setting limits
  – discipline
	• analyse the impact of legal rights on the wellbeing of parents, carers and dependants by considering the following:
	  – health and medical decisions
	  – education and schooling
	  – financial support
	• discuss how the responsibilities of parents and carers contribute to building a positive relationship with the dependant

Revision summary

The United Nation sets out the **legal rights of a child** in the Convention on the Rights of a Child. For specific rights, go to http://www.unicef.org/. The principles of the convention surround a discrimination-free environment; actions must put the child's needs first, including their life and safety and the creation of an identity through expression.

As a parent it is a responsibility to fulfil these rights. **Parents also have rights;** they have the right to make medical decisions on behalf of the child, to choose their educational background, to administer appropriate discipline and take on legal proceeding on behalf of the child.

A **carer has rights** while supporting the needs of another person. They have the right to be recognised and acknowledged for the role that they play in a dependant's life. This may mean they cannot access employment. The government has recognised this and carers have the right to financial support. Carers also have the right to respite; using either formal or informal supports will meet this right.

When a person has such influence over another, such as a parent or carer, there are **responsibilities** they must fulfil. These will align to meeting the rights of the dependant within their care. A <u>duty of care</u> is a legal obligation to maintain the health and welfare of any dependant within your care. This applies to all paid carers, formal and informal. <u>Setting limits</u> is the setting of rules which are designed to keep the dependant healthy and safe. Setting limits is aimed at maintaining the health and welfare of dependants; however, if by chance rules are broken or boundaries are pushed, a parent or carer has the responsibility to deter this behaviour from happening again by administering a consequence for the action. This is called <u>disciplining</u>. Parents and carers must ensure that discipline and subsequent actions are appropriate and are not physical.

Sample examination questions: Multiple choice

14 Which of the following are rights for parents with children who have special needs?
(A) To decide on the best means for providing care and to show love and understanding to the children
(B) To choose the school for the children and to make all decisions about medical treatment for children up to the age of 14
(C) To receive a government allowance for additional caring responsibilities and to receive support from the community
(D) To take legal proceedings on behalf of their children up to the age of 14 and to use any form of discipline to control their children
(BOS, 2012)

15 The practice of parents setting consequences for their children's behaviour relates to the
(A) rights of children.
(B) rights of parents.
(C) responsibilities of children.
(D) responsibilities of parents.
(BOSTES, 2014)

16 What responsibility is being demonstrated by working parents who ensure their children are cared for after school?
(A) Duty of care
(B) Setting limits
(C) Appropriate discipline
(D) Provision of time for children
(BOSTES, 2014)

Sample examination questions: Short answer

14 Compare how foster parents and step-parents setting limits and discipline can contribute to building a positive relationship with the dependants. (8 marks)

Both foster parents and step-parents have the legal responsibility of duty of care – the obligation to ensure the safety and security needs of a child are met. To do this, like all biological and social parents, foster carers and step-parents set limits or rules. These are designed to keep dependants safe and may range from 'stay out of the kitchen while there are things boiling' to 'you must be home before 10 p.m. on a week night' (these will vary with age). For both foster and step-parents, creating limits may become difficult as they are not the biological parents and the dependant is well aware of this. For foster parents, setting limits differs as carers may not know all of the rules a child has experienced since being in foster care – this constant changing of rules and confusion can lead the dependant to destructive behaviour, especially if the caring/parenting style is 'seen' as more authoritarian than that of previous carers. This will impact on building a positive relationship, as the dependant may feel controlled and stifled and begin to question their sense of identity, which may lead to conflict and interrupt the bonding process. This differs for step-parents as they have formed a relationship with the dependant's parent as opposed to the child. When a step-parent sets limits with too much control, the child may assume 'they want to be my parent', leading to rebelling; if no limits are set the child might assume 'well, I'm not their child, they don't care about me'. For both foster parents and step-parents, the relationship between parent/carer and child will only be positive if limits are communicated and negotiated in an open and trusting forum and with clear consequences set.

If limits are pushed or broken, consequences (discipline) will apply. As foster children are under the rule of FACS or other agencies, discipline guidelines are strict, and if they are deemed too harsh or damaging the dependant maybe removed from care. This will ruin any trust or bond built up and a positive relationship will be difficult to establish. For step-parents, again it is true that if any discipline is deemed too harsh or not in conjunction with the broken limit that the step-child may rebel and may contact the non-custodial parent and complain, again causing conflict between the step-parent and the biological parent. A household of mistrust and broken bonds will influence the positive relationships formed. For positive relationships to build, limits and discipline must be related, clearly communicated and negotiated if the dependant is capable of doing so.

15 When considering education and schooling, describe the impact legal rights of parents/carers on the wellbeing of the dependant. (4 marks)

A right is a legal entitlement; a parent has the right to choose the educational pathway and schooling of their dependant. One of a parent's responsibilities is to satisfy the educational and school rights of their child. Children have the right to free, compulsory primary education. Whether a parent chooses to send their child to a public, private, religious-based or boarding school, the child is forced to interact with peers typically of the same age; they are able to learn conflict resolution skills, social norms and communication skills, thus positively impacting on the social factors relating to wellbeing. It can have both a positive and negative impact on their emotional wellbeing, often enabling independence and confidence, but also potentially making them vulnerable to self-esteem issues and stress.

For parents choosing to send their child to a cultural or religious school, cultural factors relating to wellbeing may be satisfied. How open minded a dependant is to the teaching of culture or religion will depend on how it satisfied that area of wellbeing. Those exposed to daily prayers or weekly masses may feel spiritually connected to the school and therefore may become more involved in all aspects of the school life. This will enhance spiritual factors of wellbeing.

Types of support

Students learn about:	Students learn to:

support for parents and carers *types of support*
 • informal
    – relatives, friends, neighbours
 • formal
    – government agencies
    – community organisations
 types of support provided through formal support
 • health care
 • education
 • financial support
 • childcare
 • respite care
 • counselling
	• explain how different types of support can assist parents and carers to:
	    – prepare for their roles
	    – fulfil their responsibilities
	    – maintain their own wellbeing
	 • assess the impact accessing formal support services can have on the wellbeing of:
	    – young carers
	    – aged carers
	    – first-time parents
	    – working parents

Revision summary

When a parent or carer cannot fulfil their responsibilities, they may access *support of some type*. Formal or informal support acts as an extra set of human resources, bringing in new skills and more time to the situation. With more resources, parents and carers are more likely to be able to prepare for their roles (satisfy needs, build positive relationship and promote wellbeing), fulfil their responsibilities (setting limits, duty of care and discipline) and thus maintain their own wellbeing.

Informal support comes from the people around you such as friends, family, co-workers and neighbours. This is where you personally ask for help, or those close to you recognise there is an issue and support is offered. This support relies on the relationships built with those around you.

Formal supports are the structured organisations that are either profitable or not for profit community organisations or charities, for example a private psychologist vs. the Salvation Army Counselling service. The government also provides support through agencies such as the Department of Families and Communities and Centrelink. Support is usually from trained workers and offers either specified support or a range of specified supports.

Both young and old carers will need to access **health care** for the dependant in their care. Depending on the circumstances, health care may be covered by Medicare. However, caring for a dependant can be extremely costly, especially in rare cases. Carers may not be able to work, lowering their standard of living and influencing their wellbeing economically.

In cases like these, they may qualify for **financial support** from the formal support, Centrelink. Accessing Carers Payment and Carers Allowance may help support the basics of food, clothing and shelter. Both *young and older carers* will need to seek respite care – temporary care for the aged, ill or disabled person for periods of time. Caring for someone else is extremely draining; meeting their needs, sometimes at the expense of the carer's own needs, can take its toll physically, e.g. back pain, and emotionally, e.g. stress and conflict, influencing wellbeing. Accessing **respite care** will support both aged carers and younger carers and will allow them time away from caring responsibilities to attend doctors' appointments, to catch up with friends or to meet their leisure and recreational pursuits.

New parents may use **educational services**, such as Tresilian, Community health nurses and lactation consultants, when they need information. Supporting *new parents* is essential as many skills are new and every child is different. Specialised information from experts will ensure advice is tailored to individual needs, reducing the confusion gained from excessive advice from informal support. For new mothers experiencing post-natal depression, counselling services will provide practical strategies to ensure both mother and child are safe.

Working parents have the responsibility to ensure duty of care for their child. While they are at work they pass on that duty of care to others, such as a childcare facility. These follow strict rules in regards to safety so that working parents will have peace of mind that comes from knowing that their child is in a safe environment and that trained staff are meeting their child's immediate needs. Despite the initial impact on the working parents' wellbeing economically, emotional factors such as reduced stress, relief and peace of mind will all contribute to the satisfaction of wellbeing.

Sample examination questions: Multiple choice

17 What is the main type of assistance provided by respite care?
(A) Emotional
(B) Employment
(C) Financial
(D) Housing
(Adapted from BOS, 2013)

18 Jim is a sole parent who is struggling to pay his bills. Which of the following is most likely to provide him with financial support?
(A) A welfare agency
(B) A parenting group
(C) A childcare service
(D) A carers' support group
(BOS, 2013)

Sample examination question: Short answer

16 Explain how both formal and informal support can assist parents and carers to maintain their own wellbeing. (6 marks)

Formal support services refer to organisations that provide a structured service to those in need. Examples of formal services that support parents and carers include Tresilian and Carer NSW support groups. These support services help maintain both parents' and carers' own wellbeing by providing information and support through programs such as the Tresilian hotline for first-time parents whose emotional factors are causing ill-being. The hotline gives sound advice from trained professional on sleep, breastfeeding and general feeding issues. Accessing this advice may reduce the chances of attachment issues when breastfeeding, creating a sense of relief (emotional factors) and reducing the chance of getting mastitis (blocked milk ducts), ensuring that physical factors do not influence wellbeing. When carers feel overwhelmed by their situation and feel no one understands, they may go to a carer support group, run by Carer NSW. Sharing and talking can often be enough to boost emotional aspects of wellbeing.

An informal support is the help that is provided to an individual by friends, family or neighbours. The informal support may not have any formal training but may have knowledge through personal experience, for example a first-time parent asking a family member such as their older cousin who has had children of her own about methods of putting a newborn to sleep. This will enhance the first-time parents' wellbeing, as physical factors such as sleep are achieved, not only for the baby, but also for the parents themselves. The parent may feel more trusting of a family member, easing emotional anxiety, thus enhancing wellbeing, as family tend to share similar values. Using an informal carer, such as asking a friend whose child also has autism spectrum disorder (ASD), to look after an autistic child while the parent attends a doctor's appointment will create peace of mind, as this friend already has an understanding of these special needs. This will also reduce any physical factors influencing wellbeing, as the parent can attend the doctor's appointment or even just have time to themselves, ensuring they maintain their own sense of identity. Using informal supports ensures economic factors do not influence the overall feelings of wellbeing as no payment is required.

17 Discuss how access to respite care for an aged carer can impact on their wellbeing. (4 marks)

An aged carer is an individual who is over the age of 65 and cares for a dependant. Formal support services can impact aged carers in various ways. Respite care is one form of support that is available to aged carers. This service has become accessible to aged carers through organisations such as Home and Community Care. Respite care provides the carer with necessary breaks from the dependant when required to improve the carer's wellbeing. Both positive and negative effects on wellbeing can occur as a result of respite care. The service meets the physical factors of wellbeing, as the aged carer is able to rest and recuperate. This may be because when caring for an elderly dependant (partner), lifting to bathe and dress with already reduced mobility requires more effort.

The carer's emotional wellbeing is impacted both positively and negatively. Caring for a dependant can be emotionally draining, and respite care provides an opportunity for emotional fulfilment, reducing feelings of guilt. However, respite care can cause a negative influence on emotional factors of wellbeing. This may be due to the attachment a carer may have to a dependant, and separation may cause emotional hardship. Respite care is overall beneficial to an aged carer, although it may cause a negative influence on wellbeing.

Chapter 4

Social Impact of Technology

Social Impact of Technology should occupy approximately 25 per cent of total course time (BOS, 2013, p.41).

In our rapidly changing world, technology has played an integral role in advancements and developments in all aspects of life. In families, communities and in the workplace, technology has had an impact in both positive and negative ways.

By exploring this option, students learn about the historical development of technology and how it has changed the way in which we live. Students are then given an opportunity to analyse and discuss the reasons for the development and factors affecting the access and acceptance of technology.

Students also explore the impact of technology on lifestyle, namely the family, community and workplace. This is followed by debating and examining the issues related to information and communications technology (ICT) and the impact of emerging technologies. Finally, students choose a piece of technology and investigate issues related to technological development.

It is important to note that, like in the other options, in the final examination student responses will be assessed in relation to the rubric.

The rubric is as follows:

In your answer you will be assessed on how well you:
- demonstrate knowledge and understanding of societal influences on wellbeing relevant to the question
- apply the skills of critical thinking and analysis
- communicate ideas and information using relevant examples
- present a logical and cohesive response.

HSC option: Social Impact of Technology

Defining technology

Students learn about:	Students learn to:
defining technology • technology as hardware, e.g. appliances, gadgets, toys • technology as software, e.g. applications, databases, websites • technology as organisation of knowledge, e.g. communications, media, internet, home entertainment	• describe both primitive and complex technologies

Revision summary

Defining technology involves referring to the various examples of technology, which include **technology as hardware**, **technology as software**, and **technology as organisation of knowledge**. Within these, both primitive and complex technologies exist.

Technology can be defined as a study, system, process, program, approach, tool or piece of equipment that is used to solve, create, improve, communicate and develop.

Technology as hardware can include appliances, gadgets and toys. Hardware is any tangible tool, piece of equipment or machinery that is used to do or make something. Appliances are pieces of technology that make everyday tasks more manageable. *Primitive technology* examples may include washboards, cast iron kettles, or a bow and drill to start a fire. *Complex technology* examples could include washing machines, electric kettles and ducted air conditioners. Gadgets are small devices or tools that serve a particular purpose. *Primitive technology* examples of gadgets may include boomerangs, wooden mallets and the telegraph. *Complex technology* examples could include fishing rods, electric drills and smartphones. Toys are playthings predominately used by children for entertainment and enjoyment. *Primitive technology* examples might include knucklebones, rocking horses and wooden dolls. *Complex technology* examples could include light-up dice, Pony Cycles and Barbie dolls.

Technology as software can include applications, databases and websites. Software are programs or operating systems running a computer or other device. Applications are computer programs designed to perform a group of functions. *Primitive technology* examples include IBM PCs, Fortran and Speedcode. *Complex technology* examples could include Windows 10 and OS X Mountain Lion v10.8.5. Databases are computer mechanisms for retrieving and storing data. *Primitive technology* examples include drawer collectors and filing cabinets. *Complex technology* examples could include Oracle databases and Microsoft SQL Server. Websites are a collection of pages of information on the World Wide Web. *Primitive technology* examples include CERN and the original Yahoo! *Complex technology* examples could include Google Chrome and Amazon.

Technology as organisation of knowledge can include <u>communications,</u> <u>media, internet</u> and <u>home entertainment</u>. <u>Communications</u> are the ways in which messages are sent or retrieved. *Primitive technology* examples could include Morse code and horns. *Complex technology* examples may include Skype and email. <u>Media</u> is the means in which certain messages are sent via a form of mass communication. *Primitive technology* examples could include a printing press and a wireless. *Complex technology* examples may include podcasts and RSS feeds. Internet is a worldwide computer networking system. *Primitive technology* examples include packet networking and Advanced Research Projects Agency Network (ARPANET) link. *Complex technology* examples could include Netflix and Google. Home entertainment includes the devices and equipment used in one's home for leisure and/or recreation. *Primitive technology* examples include gramophone and video tape recorder. *Complex technology* examples could include tablets and Xbox One.

Sample examination questions: Short answer

1   **Explain how technology can be defined as organisation of knowledge.** (4 marks)

Technology as organisation of knowledge is one way in which technology can be defined. This definition encompasses the various uses of technology through which individuals communicate, use media, browse the internet and enjoy home entertainment to communicate information and improve understanding.

Communication technology, using primitive examples such a Morse code and fire signals, and complex technology, such as smartphones and email, allows individuals and groups to send and receive messages in an effective and efficient way. Technology as organisation of knowledge also includes media, which can be the expression of a message on a large scale. Primitive examples, which are still sometimes used today, include posters and a wireless/radio. Far greater is the impact and reach of our modern, more complex technologies such as podcasts and social media like Facebook or Twitter.

Another form that affects the way in which technology can be defined as organisation of knowledge is the powerful information tool that is the internet. The internet has come a long way from the early experimental days of using packet networking to worldwide reaches, to uses of the internet for almost anything from online shopping to directions from one destination to the next using Google Maps.

Finally, entertainment technology is another example to demonstrate the definition of technology as organisation of knowledge. Home entertainment, including primitive examples like a gramophone and video tape recorder, can be used for the discovery of news and the enjoyment of entertainment programs. Complex examples such as iPads and gaming consoles such as Xbox can be used for reading, games, watching film clips and listening to music.

Historical perspectives

Students learn about:	Students learn to:
historical perspectives • the Digital Revolution • the Information Age	• outline how the nature and use of information and communication technology has evolved • examine data from the Australian Bureau of Statistics (ABS) to compare trends in household use of information and communication technology over time

Revision summary

The *historical perspectives* of **the Digital Revolution** and **the Information Age** have contributed to the nature and use of how information and communication technology has evolved.

The experimentation and technological development during the 1950s, 1960s and 1970s paved the way for an increase in the presence of personal computers and the internet in the 1980s. These increases have led to **the Digital Revolution** and can be described as change from analogue, electronic and mechanical technology to digital technology.

The Information Age is a period in time that is by characterised by computer use and is associated with **the Digital Revolution**. It is commonly known as the Digital or Computer Age. This era has sparked changes to industry, business, communities and families in the way technology is researched, developed and used to transfer information, access information, communicate locally and globally, and perform everyday tasks.

Both **the Digital Revolution** and **the Information Age** have also contributed to the nature and use of how information and communication technology has evolved by creating global platforms for networking all across the world.

Data from the Australian Bureau of Statistics can be *examined* to *compare trends in household use of information and communication technology over time*. Trends indicate that technology use and ownership is continuing to increase, with 83% of all Australian households having access to internet in their home and 81% of households stating that they use the internet every day of the week (ABS, 2014). This has increased dramatically from 1998 where only 16% had home internet access (ABS, 1999).

Sample examination questions: Short answer

2   Outline how the use of information and communication technology has evolved since the start of the Information Age. (4 marks)

The Information Age is a period in history after the Industrial Revolution that is associated with the Digital Revolution and is characterised by computerisation. Information and communication technology has evolved dramatically since the start of this period and its prime mover is the internet. The internet, which is a system of interconnected networks, has made global communication possible and has changed family, community and workplace relationships, structures and systems.

In the early years of the Information Age, information and communication was made possible by packet switching for the ARPANET. This system meant that multiple separate networks could be joined into a network of networks, used initially by governments, militaries and universities.

Developments made 20 years later to various networks meant that from ARPANET, encoded messages through electronic mail or email were used to communicate a digital message over the internet. This feature of information and communication technology meant that messages could be sent electronically and included three components: the message envelope, the message header, and the message body.

Fast-forwarding another 20 years sees the latest evolution in information and communication technology through Cloud computing, which is internet-based and offers shared processing resources and data to computers and other devices on-demand through platforms such as Google Docs or Amazon Web Services.

Reasons for the development of technology

Students learn about:	Students learn to:

reasons for the development of technology
• improve upon existing technology
• economic benefit
• consumer demand and human needs
• social betterment
• the global community
• response to social problems
	• analyse how technology has emerged within the following contexts:
	  – transport
	  – communication
	  – consumer services

Revision summary

There are many **reasons for the development of technology**, which include **to improve upon existing technology, economic benefit, consumer demand and human needs, social betterment, the global community, and response to social problems**. These developments have been made within the contexts of *transport*, *communication* and *consumer services*.

By being able to **improve on existing technology** you might see *transport* changes, with the emergence of economic and environmentally friendly fuel use, rechargeable cars and safety with reversing cameras. Changes to *communication* technology could include size of portable devices, durability and functionality. *Consumer services* changes might mean that the response to help is available in different forms, times and is easier to access at home.

There is an **economic benefit** to many of the developments in technology. Within *transport* there may be an economic benefit to the manufacturer such using robots to build cars or saving money on fuel for a consumer. The development of *communication* platforms such as Google Hangout has meant that businesses are rewarded with an economic benefit, as they may not have to fly their employees interstate for a meeting. *Consumer services* also see an economic benefit with the use of call centres or online customer support where they save on printing, employee efficiency, and the need for physical offices.

Consumer demand and human needs can lead to changes in *transport* where there may be more of a demand for environmentally friendly cars or cars that have good sound systems with iPod connectivity and Bluetooth. The necessity for people to have access to mobile *communication* has meant that mobile phones are constantly being updated to be more portable, durable, multi-function and affordable for people of all ages and walks of life. The need for consumers to work full-time in a variety of patterns of work has meant that *consumer services* need to make themselves available twenty-four hours a day to meet these needs to access support or information.

New technologies have often been developed due to **social betterment.** Examples in *transport* might include the community's continuing awareness of the damaging effects of fuel on the environment or the introduction of hybrid cars to reduce the dependence on fossil fuels. *Communication* technology can improve relationships with the use of networking services like Skype, FaceTime or video conferencing (although technology use can also impact on interpersonal relationships negatively). The availability and ease of use of _consumer services_ will continue to be developed further due to the importance of positive reviews and feedback in such a competitive marketplace.

The global community is impacted through the various developments made to _transport._ Low emission fuels used in various modes of transport have been chosen to improve air quality and reduce pollution significantly. Improvements made in the weight and size of bicycles (and their demand for trendiness and fitness) has come out of the environmental impact of cars on the road. Strengthening global networks and relationships can result from improvements in _communication_ technology. The availability and accessibility of forums or instant messenger offered by various _consumer services_ were designed to increase business relationships and connections throughout the world.

Some technologies have been developed as a result of a **response to social problems.** With regard to _transport,_ the installation of safety glass in buses and cameras has evolved out of improving the safety of both travellers and bus drivers. Improvements made to _communication_ technology may be apparent due to the need of many individuals to 'fit in' by having a phone or due to safety concerns travelling to and from school or work. Online help by _consumer services,_ especially the use of help lines such as Tresillian or information lines, has come about due to constant support needed by some individuals in our community. They may either be suffering an illness or do not have informal support at home.

Sample examination questions: Short answer

3   **Describe reasons for the development of technology.** (6 marks)
     (Adapted from BOS, 2010)

There are various reasons for the development of technology, including to improve on existing technologies, respond to consumer demand and human needs, and achieve social betterment.

Some technological developments have been made for the improvement of existing technologies. These improvements can be characterised by economical changes and could be evident through the production of more economical fuel consumption cars or sensor dryers. An additional characteristic for the development of technology is the improvement to create more environmentally friendly choices. One such example is the development of solar or rechargeable cars, which give off fewer emissions into the atmosphere. Another feature that could lead to technological developments is the portability and durability of technology. This feature is evident in the constant size change of smartphones and possibly the development of the Apple Watch into products that are more portable and durable in nature.

Another reason for the development of technology is due to consumer demand and human needs. Consumers are keeping technological developers on their toes by purchasing the latest and greatest version of a piece of technology. A clear example of this is through the release of newer versions of Apple iPhones. Consumers put these products in high demand, often pre-ordering or lining up to be one of the first people to own the latest version. Human needs being satisfied is another reason for technological developments. In the case of consumer services, many organisations offer after hours services, support and shopping to make them more accessible to individuals in full-time work.

An additional reason for the development of technology is for social betterment. A feature of social betterment is the reduction of time by using labour-saving devices. By using a dishwasher to wash the dishes, individuals and family members can spend time relaxing, doing other household duties or interacting with family and friends. Another aspect of social betterment could be the improvements made to information and communication technology to allow individuals feel better connected with technologies such as Skype, FaceTime and social media such as Instagram.

Factors affecting access to and acceptance of technology

Students learn about:	Students learn to:
factors affecting access to and acceptance of technology • age • culture • education • economic status • disability • geographical location • gender • religion	• discuss how each of the factors may impact on an individual's access to and acceptance of technology

Revision summary

There are a number of **factors affecting access to and acceptance of technology**, which will either help or hinder individuals and groups. These include **age**, **culture**, **education**, **economic status**, **disability**, **geographical location**, **gender** and **religion**. _Each of the factors may impact on an individual's access to and acceptance of technology._

Due to the **age** variance in different generations, individuals tend to view technology differently because of their awareness, familiarity, usability and knowledge of technology.

Culture can pose varying language barriers, restrictions and affordability issues, but can also allow languages and customs to be better understood by other cultures via knowledge shared on the internet and social media.

Rapid changes in technology have meant that educational institutions have used advancements to enhance **education**. This has led to an increase in usage in worldwide classrooms through face-to-face, online learning and distance education. Consequently, this has placed additional pressure on learners, their families and communication companies to have the latest hardware and software as well as the training and maintenance for technology.

Economic status can impact on the type, timing and connectivity of technology. Owning the latest and greatest may put undue pressure and stress on individuals and groups to keep up with societal expectations.

An individual's **disability** can be managed more effectively with technology with specialised medical equipment and procedures. Conversely, modifications might need to be made to certain technological devices for people with a disability to access.

Geographic location has been impacted by technology, from allowing rural communities greater social connection and opportunities for online learning, to connecting global marketplaces, online shopping and access to online support and services.

An individual's **gender** may affect their access to certain technological products and services advertised in the media as they may use techniques to win over the buyer. In addition, there may be certain gender expectations around the successful use and suitability of certain pieces of technology.

Religion may also provide barriers to the use of technology; alternatively, technology can expose individuals to varying religions across communities. There may be some religions that restrict the access and use of technological devices and procedures. On the other hand, there could be religions that embrace technology, using it in a number of ways for spreading their faith, engaging their community, celebrating ceremonies or undertaking administrative tasks.

Sample examination questions: Short answer

4   **Explain why the access and acceptance of technology varies**. (6 marks)
    (Adapted from BOS, 2013)

Access and acceptance of technology varies due to a number of factors, including economic status, geographical location and disability.

Economic status is one of the reasons why access and acceptance of technology varies. Low-income families have limited monetary resources available to them and often technological purchases such as a desktop computer or broadband internet access are seen as a want or luxury. They may accept technology, but their access to it is significantly limited, which may cause pressure and tension within the family. Individuals in a family with a high economic status may be more likely to have access to technology as they have more disposable income accessible to them and could possibly have greater educational and entertainment opportunities available.

In addition, an individual's geographical location has an impact on access and acceptance of technology, although this difference might not be as evident as it was in the past. Some access to technology is limited in rural/regional areas due to service or internet coverage away from major exchanges. Therefore, this may lead to frustration for individuals and as a result there may be a reluctance to use technology and accept new technologies due to negative experiences. Conversely, individuals working or living remotely may in fact have positive experiences of technology due to their location. For example, teachers working with students in distance education rely heavily on technology for learning; their effective access to it is paramount for the successful achievement of student outcomes. This can have a positive effect on acceptance of technology as they are so experienced using it, they will be open to new uses to make their job more effective and efficient.

Disability is an additional factor affecting access and acceptance of technology. Specialised equipment, devices and gadgets may need to be purchased for daily living of people with disabilities, but the access may be significantly expensive, resulting in financial pressure on family members such as taking out personal loans to pay for equipment. Technology is often embraced and accepted for people with a disability due to its importance for safety, care and monitoring. For example, motorised wheelchairs are advancements of a push wheelchair and make mobilisation, independence and care a lot easier for both a carer and/or a person with a disability.

The impact of technology on lifestyle

Students learn about:	Students learn to:
the impact of technology on lifestyle *technologies and the family* • household technology • information and communication technology • entertainment technology	• explore how household technology contributes to the wellbeing of individuals within families • critically analyse the impact of technology on interpersonal relationships within families

Revision summary

The impact of technology on lifestyle can be explored through *technologies and the family, technologies and the community,* and *technology and the workplace.*

Technologies and the family include **household technology, information and communication technology,** and **entertainment technology**.

Household technology has been positively impacted by the introduction of labour-saving devices such as washing machines, dishwashers, dryers and vacuum cleaners. Cooking utensils and gadgets as well as online shopping have also had a positive impact on families. These products and services have freed up time for families to manage their multiple commitments and have contributed to the social and emotional wellbeing of individuals within families, as well having a positive *impact of technology on interpersonal relationships within families.*

Information and communication technology allows families to stay connected, capture memories, access information, engage in social media and manage weekly routines. These aspects make managing resources more effective and can also become a positive *impact of technology on interpersonal relationships within families* through emailing, messaging and using social media to share news, stories, photos and experiences with family members, especially those living remotely, interstate or overseas. Conversely, there could be a negative *impact of technology on interpersonal relationships within families* as it may cause families to develop unhealthy technology habits through the constant use of social media, inability to switch off due to 24/7 accessibility, reliance on the internet and the desire to keep up with the latest trends and technology.

Entertainment technology can provide much needed relaxation and recuperation from the fast-paced lives many families in today's society lead. Tablets, game consoles, desktop computers, smartphones, sound systems, MP3 players, radios, televisions, DVD/Blu-ray players and the like can be used for viewing movies, performances, documentaries, television and clips; listening to podcasts, radio broadcasts, music and audio books; playing console or interactive games; and reading books, blogs, and stories. By enjoying time engaging with entertainment technology either individually or together it can improve the social connection and bond between family members, therefore having a positive *impact of technology on interpersonal relationships within* *families*. On the other hand, it can have a negative *impact of technology on interpersonal relationships within families* as members may spend hours connected, develop obsessions, be affected cognitively, be diagnosed with visual or auditory issues, become distracted, and possibly be in financial debt due to excess use.

Sample examination questions: Short answer

5   **Examine how household technology contributes to the wellbeing of individuals within families**. (6 marks)

It is important to consider that many examples of household technology allow family members to expend less energy and effort. Dryers and automatic vacuum cleaners contribute positively to wellbeing physically as they require less physical exertion and energy. For example, a mother may choose to use a dryer to ease the strain she would place on her body if she were to carry a heavy basket full of washing out and put it on the line. Using a dryer may also prevent family members from ironing their clothes, as creases tend to reduce in the dryer. In turn, this contributes to positive wellbeing socially as the parent may have more time to spend with their young children.

What also needs to be noted is that a reduction in costs is noticeable as a result of using fridges/freezers and carefully packing food and drinks, leading to highly efficient and effective storage. This influences wellbeing economically in that money and time is saved by freezing food such as meat bought in bulk and leftovers for future meals. As a result, individuals within families may have more leisure time available.

Dishwashers would be another example of a household technology that reduces costs. Many types of this appliance have been developed with high water efficient and energy ratings. This results in improved economic wellbeing as money is saved on water and electricity bills. Individuals in a family, such as adolescents, would also improve their wellbeing physically instead of hand washing after meals.

Online shopping saves time and energy. This contributes positively to wellbeing both physically and economically as a family member such as a sole parent can shop in the comfort of their own home instead of attempting to find a car park, choose, pay and pack their groceries. Family members can then spend more time with each other rather than go shopping, thus impacting their wellbeing socially. Air conditioners could also save individuals' time by using a motor to cool the house down rather than an open window or fan. This use also contributes positively to wellbeing physically and emotionally because family members would feel more relaxed and productive in a cool home.

Sample examination questions: Extended response

1   Discuss the impact of entertainment technology on interpersonal relationships in families. (15 marks) (Adapted from BOS, 2011)

Entertainment technology can have a positive and detrimental impact on interpersonal relationships in families.

One positive impact of entertainment technology on interpersonal relationships in families can result through bonding. Consequently, this can create a sense of closeness and togetherness where families can enjoy being together and sharing special moments. This can be experienced while sitting on the couch together as a family to watch a movie played on either a DVD player, Blu-ray or via Apple TV. Watching a movie together can also promote physical closeness where the family may sit close together, possibly sharing a blanket or bean bag while enjoying the entertainment provided by the movie. It is in moments like these that children, either young or adult, may ask questions, seek advice from parents or learn from each other. This may enhance their wellbeing socially, as they feel like they belong, and emotionally, as they have a positive self-esteem in feelings of trust and understanding in the intimate family moment shared.

Furthermore, entertainment technology can help create memories, and this impacts positively on interpersonal relationships in families. Family members either in smaller groups or as a whole may enjoy the entertainment provided by gaming consoles such as Nintendo Wii, Microsoft Xbox and Sony PlayStation. Some families may choose to create a fun family competition where they participate against each other either individually or in teams such as those provided by Nintendo Wii Sports. This may a create fun and energetic atmosphere which could impact positively on other experiences as a family and lead to family members spending more time together and seeking advice from each other. This therefore impacts on their wellbeing physically, especially if they have enjoyed interactive games, emotionally, as they may develop a good self-concept, and socially, as they develop a sense of belonging.

In addition, various entertainment technology impacts positively on interpersonal relationships in families by creating a relaxing or happy atmosphere. This can occur through music, which may be used online through applications such as iTunes, CDs, or MP3 players like iPods. Music can influence any mood, and by using music positively around the home, families may develop a sense of togetherness, inner peace and/or a sense of fun. They may choose to discuss or assist in making music choices, but the uses of music can have favourable impacts on wellbeing through calmness and energy, impacting on wellbeing physically and possibly spiritually as the family may experience a sense of purpose as a family unit.

In contrast to this is the detrimental impact that entertainment technology has on interpersonal family relationships. The first issue that may arise is hostility and aggression. This can stem from the sort of language, graphics and themes offered by online gaming. Family members using this sort of technology are often being exposed to very explicit messages, which could have a negative impact on interrelationships and may impact on wellbeing physically, through violence and mistreatment, and emotionally, through inappropriate language leading to anxiety, fear and lowered self-esteem.

Another significant impact on interpersonal relationships in families when using entertainment technology is decreased attention span and increased distractions and interruptions. This can result via the use of video clips, YouTube clips and apps. Colours, loud noises, flashes and animations used by these examples of technology can impact on brain function and processing. This would therefore have an impact on communication in families, as when important messages are being shared, retrieved or relayed, family members may be distracted by such technology. This idea of multi-tasking divides attention and could also contribute to feelings of ill-being for family members, especially emotionally and socially, as they may feel neglected, ignored and rejected.

Associated with this feeling of ill-being could possibly be the tension, stress, anxiety and lack of sleep developed by using some forms of entertainment technology. These feelings can impact on interpersonal relationships in fairly significant ways. Entertainment technology such as television programs, box sets and reality television can create feelings of addiction, which can cause anxiety and lead to isolation. This has an impact on the wellbeing of family socially, through the lack of connectedness and companionship, as well as emotionally, through lowered self-esteem and moodiness.

Technologies and the community

Students learn about:	Students learn to:
technologies and the community • education and training • transport and travel • health and medicine • food • leisure and entertainment	• explore how technology contributes to productive communities • critically examine the impact of technology on community health and wellbeing

Revision summary

Technologies and the community include **education and training**, **transport and travel**, **health and medicine**, **food**, and **leisure and entertainment**.

Technology has made **education and training** more accessible, productive, available, differentiated, equitable and interactive through the variety of courses and opportunities offered to members of the community.

Transport and travel have seen changes in technology to the mode, operation, speed, distance, time, fuel efficiency, emissions, security, delays and destination choices made by individuals within the community.

The technology used in **health and medicine** have created life-changing advancements in developing, preventing, diagnosing, treating, training, reproducing and improving medical conditions, surgery techniques, diseases, injuries, defects, health and cosmetic issues.

Food has been impacted by technology in growing, developing, cropping, watering, marketing, modifying, sterilising, packaging, freezing, delivering and storing of products available at home, on farms, in grocery stores, at fast food outlets, markets, cafes, restaurants, in hospitals and in the hospitality industry.

The availability, accessibility and choice in **leisure and entertainment** have meant that individuals can enjoy leisure and recreation in new and exciting ways, which can bring communities closer together. Some new leisure and entertainment technologies entail significant ongoing costs and updates.

Technology contributes to productive communities through the availability, affordability and accessibility of various devices, products and services. Robots, highly advanced machines and specialised equipment in factories have saved businesses time, money, productivity, incidents, accidents and injuries.

The impact of technology on community health and wellbeing in a positive manner can be attributed to advancements in medical equipment, improvements in diagnosis, rehabilitation, disease prevention and cure, treatment, awareness of wellness programs, availability of nutritional guidelines, and the development of new health and entertainment/leisure equipment/devices. Negatively, technology can impact on community health and wellbeing through increasingly sedentary behaviour, poor food habits, obsessions with technology, environmental concerns, financial hardship, societal pressure, and dangerous or inappropriate social media practices.

Sample examination questions: Short answer

6   **Examine how food and travel technology contributes to productive communities.** (6 marks)

Food and travel technology contributes positively to productive communities by saving time, improving energy and reducing costs.

The food industry has developed many appliances, products and services to improve the storage, production and preservation of various foods. Recycled and compact packaging contributes to productive communities by saving manufacturers' time, money and energy on their packaged goods. It could also prevent products from being damaged and lead to businesses being more productive for these companies as consumers or distributors are not returning their products. Packaging, such as foil bags or zip seals, and the technology used to produce preservatives and pesticides contributes to productive communities as consumers do not have to destroy the spoilt goods and this therefore saves them the time (and money) of replacing them at the shops.

In addition, the machinery and preservation in preparing raw foods contributes to productive communities. Machines used to cut vegetables or products for frozen foods reduce time, labour and costs for food companies. As a result, these companies can pass the savings on to consumers. The technology used to develop products such as these also contributes to productive communities, as frozen meals and frozen vegetables can save individuals, groups and families a significant amount of time in washing, cutting and cooking for meal preparation. This means that individuals will be more productive in other areas as they manage their multiple commitments.

Transport technology has evolved and there are many areas that have contributed to improving time, energy and costs to generate productive communities. Fuel efficiency in cars, motorbikes, trains, buses and aeroplanes has significantly improved and become more environmentally friendly. This has also meant that communities are more productive as they do not need to replenish fuel as often or suffer the environmental issues associated with the use of many fuels. Using services has also created technological advancements to increase the productivity of communities. Apps for timetables, online bookings, check-ins and passport scanners has made using transport more efficient and easier. Although the development and introduction of these technologies may have been costly, it is outweighed by the time and energy saved by consumers. Transport technology has been developed with safety in mind. App alerts for traffic or late trains, reversing cameras, hands-free kits, seat belt alerts and electric ramps have improved the safety, wellbeing and productivity of individuals and communities.

Technologies and the workplace

Students learn about:	Students learn to:
technologies and the workplace	
• safety technology	• assess the degree to which
• information and communication technology	technology impacts on:
	– workplace safety
• structure of the workplace	– work/life balance
– health and safety	– career pathways
– equipment	• evaluate the rights and
– efficiency	responsibilities of employers and
– flexibility	employees in adopting technology in
– education and training	the workplace
• introduction of technology into the workplace	

Revision summary

Technologies and the workplace encompasses issues relating to **safety technology**; **information and communication technology**; **structure of the workplace**: *health and safety, equipment, efficiency, flexibility, education and training*; and the **introduction of technology into the workplace**.

Safety technology includes using specialised safety equipment, adopting protocols and introducing procedures to ensure the safety of the employer and employee is maintained. This significantly *impacts workplace safety* through the use of things such as ergonomic office equipment, computer programs, shut-off switches, digital logs and computerised controls. The *rights and responsibilities of employers and employees in adopting technology in the workplace* are to check, maintain and service equipment; engage with the most up-to-date safety education and training; and use safety technology in a safe manner to reduce hazards, eliminate injury and prevent death in accordance with the *Work Health and Safety Act 2011*.

Information and communication technology allows employers and employees to learn, connect, share and collaborate in their roles in the workplace by using search engines on the internet to build knowledge, emailing to share and receive information, and planning and developing projects using Google Drive. This significantly *impacts work/life balance*, as employers and employees can use information and communication technology at home by having remote access, checking emails, staying connected through programs like LinkedIn and finishing work at home by accessing databases offsite. This could have detrimental effects to family relationships as well as physical, emotional and social wellbeing. The *rights and responsibilities of employers and employees in adopting technology in the workplace* is to develop practices to safely use information and communication technology while maintaining a positive work/life balance.

The **structure of the workplace** through *health and safety, equipment, efficiency, flexibility, education and training* allows employees and employers to use technology within systems, practices, protocols and *Health and safety* guidelines and legislation provided by Safe Work Australia and the Fair Work Act.

Equipment needs to be used in a safe and ethical manner alongside specialised training, servicing and updating. Technology in the workplace, such as robotics and tailored software packages, has led to greater *efficiency* of tasks, reducing time and money for companies. The *flexibility* of the workplace through patterns of work, such as working remotely, allows employees to use home offices and programs such as Skype, FaceTime and Google Hangout to fulfil their workplace duties. *Education and training* is essential for the development, implementation, learning and use of technological programs, devices, equipment, services and updating/retraining. These all affect the *workplace safety* and *work/life balance* of employers and employees, although the *rights and responsibilities of employers and employees in adopting technology in the workplace* need to be transparent and understood.

The **introduction of technology into the workplace** is not a new concept, but the speed at which technological advancements are being made means that workplaces are constantly under pressure to keep up with the latest technology. This can cause issues in updating costs, resistance to change, fear, as well as education, training and retraining of employees. This also considerably *impacts workplace safety* through the introduction of education and training to use the new technology. This means that the *rights and responsibilities of employers and employees in adopting technology in the workplace* need to be fully examined before the new technology can be adopted. Various *career pathways* can also be developed and explored with the introduction of new technologies.

Sample examination questions: Extended response

2   **Analyse how the use of technology has affected work efficiency and training and education.** (15 marks) (BOSTES, 2014)

Technology has affected work efficiency and training and education in several ways and has had both positive and negative effects on wellbeing. These positive implications for efficiency include streamlining, flexibility, communication and collaboration. Negative implications potentially include robotics, isolation, personal use and costs. The impact of technology on training and education offers positive implications through online learning, courses, retraining and specialised training. The negative implications of these include stress/fear, loss of jobs, costs and reliability.

Efficiency in the workplace has improved significantly as a result of technology, often saving companies and organisations substantial time and money. Technology has streamlined processes in the workplace, which has led to efficiency. This can be seen through the use of computers, machines and software to process information instead of hand writing orders, data, tests, results or complaints. This also results in more efficient sharing, storage and analysis of data. For example, in a grocery store, employees can use barcode readers to place orders into head office for low stock items. These orders can be sent directly to the supplier rather than hand writing the order, filling out more paperwork and then either posting it by mail (or fax) or handing it to a distributor to process at their end. This saves grocery stores and the supplier time and money, which would contribute to their wellbeing emotionally, through a sense of self-satisfaction that they have been productive, and impact economic wellbeing, as they have saved the company significant time and money by streamlining the process by using technology.

Streamlined processes are often characterised by an increase in the adoption of specialised machinery and, more recently, robotics. The use of such technology offers some detrimental effects to employees, possibly through the restructure of responsibilities, redundancy or complete retrenchment as robots or specialised machines replace the tasks that were one completed by employees. An example of this has been evident in the Australian car manufacturing industry, where thousands of jobs were lost to robots. This demonstrates a negative effect of technology in work efficiency where wellbeing of the employee and their family may be diminished economically, socially and emotionally when they are retrenched or made redundant.

In addition to this, technology has led to efficiency through an increase in flexible work patterns such as working remotely. Advancements in information and communication technology have really changed the way we see work. By using laptops, tablets and other forms of technology in a home office, many employees can perform the same duties they would ordinarily do while actually at work. Employers are allowing more flexibility in the way their employees may work to improve efficiency. This has resulted in saving the employee time travelling into work and generated the saving of money that they might ordinarily allocate to renting office spaces/equipment and travel expenses. This increase in flexible work patterns has improved wellbeing emotionally. Employees tend to be more satisfied as they do not have to travel into work and can use the flexibility at home to manage their multiple commitments, such as being able to pick up children from school, as long as they complete the necessary tasks/hours allocated. If the employee's needs are met and they have a high level of wellbeing, then they will feel positive about working, be more motivated and work hard for the company, therefore impacting on the wellbeing of the employer both economically and emotionally.

Subsequently, the increase in flexible work patterns due to efficiency of technology may have an impact on the face-to-face contact with other employees and business contacts. If employees are not regularly at the workplace, then they may miss out on messages distributed verbally and the social connection of the workplace. This could therefore lead to isolation and impact wellbeing emotionally, as employees feel depressed and have a lowered self-esteem, and also impact socially as they are not socialising or having lunch with other employees.

Improved communication can also be the result of efficiency in the workplace through technology. Systems used to send, receive and distribute messages can have an impact on the speed or time taken to complete tasks. Examples that have led to this improvement in efficiency include laptops and tablets used for iMessage or messenger, email, smartphones through text messages and FaceTime, telephone systems, dashboard announcements, and communication platforms such as Skype and Google Hangout. Improved communication can also result through promoting collaboration via the use of platforms such as those offered by cloud computing including Google Docs. The ease of distribution and the reach and response of information is greatly improved by the technology available today for workplaces to utilise, which in turn saves money, energy and time and leads to efficiency. Improved communication may enhance wellbeing socially, as employees feel both connected and up to date with information, as well as emotionally, as they can achieve their daily tasks/responsibilities and contribute to an efficient workplace.

Negative implications of improved communication in the workplace as a result of technology being efficient may stem from the personal uses that may surface as a consequence. Employees may begin to use their laptops or tablets for personal use either at home or in the workplace. They could also take advantage of their smartphone by texting while at work or making lengthy personal phones calls with the work phone or on their mobile phone. Internet browsing, online shopping and social media use may become apparent with the use of devices used for communication such as desktop computers, laptops, tablets and smartphones. This use has a negative impact on the wellbeing of the employees in an economic sense, as it would cost organisations substantial amounts in fees as well as time and money lost.

As it has been established, technology has affected various aspects of the workplace and training, and education is an additional area that has been impacted. Online training, online workshops and online courses have all been more available and affordable through the use of technology. Workplaces can use online learning for the long-term benefit of their workplace and the training and the education of their employees. Training, workshops and courses can also be attended at home via the use of technology, which in turn would be cost and time-effective for employers. For example, many workplaces can now participate in mandatory Workplace Health and Safety online training developed and delivered/offered by training companies. Employers can save thousands of dollars and many hours using this form of training, rather than face-to-face training that can cost significantly more. This has positive implications for wellbeing emotionally and economically as both the employee and employer can feel that training is occurring in a more efficient and effective manner. This also has positive implications as work time is not lost or significantly impacted and there may be more flexibility in the pace that training is being covered, thus improving the learning and education of the employee.

Using technology for online training, workshops and courses may generate some negative implications. This is evident through the overabundance of training and education courses available and consequently the reliability of these courses can be questioned. Some companies see them as moneymaking schemes and develop online training without the experience or expertise in the industry that the training is designed for. In addition, there are some training, education and retraining courses offered online that may in fact be more costly for participants as there are few regulations that training companies have to adhere to or costs associated with licences to have the training software offered by the workplace. In turn, this impacts on wellbeing emotionally and economically as the training and education that might be organised may be inappropriate and the employee will not feel like they have gained the necessary knowledge and skills required to carry out their responsibilities, subsequently negatively impacting employers also.

The purchase, installation and use of new technological devices, gadgets, appliances and systems also has an impact of training and education. Specialised training and education needs to be developed and presented in order to train and educate employees and their employers for the safe, efficient and effective use of new products and systems. This training needs to be delivered by the manufacturers or affiliated associates so employees receive the information and skills to use the technology in their roles and responsibilities. For example, if a new telephone system is being installed, employees need to receive adequate training and education in using the system efficiently and effectively to continue to communicate within the workplace and with their stakeholders. This impacts wellbeing emotionally and socially as employees will feel a sense of collegiality, accomplishment and increased self-esteem.

With the introduction of new technology there may be other negative implications that result. The training and education may cause stress, fear or reluctance amongst employees because it is unknown to them or they are learning something for the first time. This may impact on their approach to the training and education they are receiving and spread to other employees, which would subsequently impact on the important information that is being attempted to communicate to them. This therefore has negative impacts on wellbeing: socially, as teamwork may be affected, emotionally, as self-esteem could diminish, and economically, as possible costs could be inflicted by the organisation/company to retrain employees.

Evidence has been provided that work efficiency training and education and associated wellbeing have been affected by technology. Implications were positive through streamlined processes, an increase in flexible work patterns, improved communication, online learning and specialised training. Subsequent negative implications included the introduction of robotics, isolation, personal uses, reliability and stress/fear.

Technological development

Students learn about:	Students learn to:
technological development *issues related to information and communication technology* • privacy and safety • security of information • accuracy of information • information overload • copyright	• debate the issues related to the development of information and communication technologies

Revision summary

Technological development has led to *issues related to information and communication technology*. These include **privacy and safety**, **security of information**, **accuracy of information**, **information overload** and **copyright**.

When sensitive information is shared or exposed via the internet, via social media, in emails or hacked, **privacy and safety** issues can result which may compromise the safety, security, identity and wellbeing of individuals and groups. There is also software such as anti-virus and security codes and hardware such as surveillance cameras and automatic gates that can also protect individuals and property.

Security of information is also threatened by the use of technology. It is important for people to be savvy in the storing, sharing and collaboration of information as there is software, hardware, individuals and groups that can hack and attack information.

Individuals of all ages and technological experience need to be aware of the **accuracy of information** they receive via the internet, social media, in podcasts, e-newsletters, online forums, blogs and websites such as Wikipedia. The reliability of information can be enhanced using current, government recommended and unbiased sources.

With an abundance of technology available there is the potential for **information overload**. This can be through the availability of information online, data received through spam email and messages, choices in software and constant updates to hardware available on the market.

Technology has completely changed the nature of **copyright** in all communities, both in person and virtually. The protection of resources such as books, music, photography, movies, art, advertising and student assignments is at risk due to the availability and access of these sources. Although there are legislation, programs and fines associated with this behaviour, individuals and groups continue to breach copyright laws and regulations by downloading, sharing, duplicating and plagiarising.

Sample examination questions: Short answer

7   **Outline how technological developments have led to computer crime.**
(4 marks) (BOS, 2013)

Technological developments have led to an increase in computer crime. Technological developments in hacking machines, spam, cyber cams and software programs continue to be exploited by illegal means in the breach of security of information. Criminals can access databases, decode, hack into computers, download emails and access personal information via illegal means. This may lead to fraud, bank and/or identification theft, all of which are against the law.

Additionally, criminals may engage in illegal behaviour through breaching copyright by selling illegal or counterfeit copies of books, CDs, movies and games. Technological developments in recording devices, viruses, counter-devices, manipulation of files and downloading software have led to computer crime and illegal production, sharing, distribution, selling and sharing of various goods.

Impact of emerging technologies

Students learn about:	Students learn to:
impact of emerging technologies • ethics • equity and access • health and safety • economic • environmental • education and learning	• examine various emerging technologies and predict the potential impact of their development

Revision summary

With research, development, advancements and improvements being made in research fields, there will be an *impact of emerging technologies.* These areas of impact include **ethics, equity and access, health and safety, economic, environmental**, and **education and learning**.

Many new developments made in technology may question an individual's **ethics** and morals. *Emerging technologies* such as surrogacy and genetic engineering may question the ethical beliefs of individuals, and *the potential impact of their development* might include questions about the rights of the parents and the interference of the natural conception of life.

The **equity and access** of technology means that individuals should have the right to gain access to technology no matter their location or socioeconomic status. *Emerging technologies* such as the National Broadband Network, small tablets and wearable devices have meant that *the potential impact of their development* might include greater accessibility to the various features of the internet and portability of data.

Various advancements in technology have positively impacted **health and safety**. *Emerging technologies* such as stem cell research and autonomous cars may mean that the *potential impact of their development* might be very positive through the treatment of a range of injuries or diseases and reduced traffic collisions and congestions.

Although there are significant costs associated with the research and development of new technology, long-term **economic** benefits are often the driving forces behind production. *Emerging technologies* such as 3D printing and improvements to desalination plants may create a positive *potential impact of their development*. This might include the relatively inexpensive production of a small numbers of parts and reduction in costs associated with water and electricity bills.

Researchers are well aware of the detrimental effects of resources on our world, so they have considered the **environmental** impact by the development of *emerging technologies* such as in vitro meat and solar power. The *potential impact of their development* might include reducing the large amounts of methane gas produced by animals that are bred for slaughter and the replacement of traditional fossil fuels.

Advancements and developments in technology have had a meaningful impact on **education and learning**. _Emerging technologies_ such as cloud computing and mobile technology have led to an engaging _potential impact of their development_ by creating online collaboration through the sharing of knowledge and ideas as well as creating opportunities for differentiation and self-directed learning.

Sample examination questions: Short answer

8   **Outline an equity issue affecting access to technology.** (4 marks)
(Adapted from BOS, 2010)

An equity issue affecting access to an emerging technology is 'bring your own device' (BYOD) in educational settings. Equity means that individuals would have equal access. Unfortunately, due to the costs associated with purchasing a portable device such as a laptop or tablet, it may not be equitable to request students to bring their own device to school or university. Setting classwork or homework using their own device where they have to download and watch video clips, browse the internet or contribute to a shared task may not be possible, especially when families may be sharing a device or not even own one.

9   **Predict the potential impact of the development of a range of emerging technologies**. (6 marks)

The development of emerging technologies has the potential for both favourable and detrimental impact on individuals, families and communities. One of the areas that will be impacted by emerging technologies is ethics and morals. The values and standards of individuals and groups will be tested with the use of emerging technologies such as surrogacy and genetic engineering.
Surrogacy is when a woman carries a baby for a couple or single person by using IVF or other technology. On a favourable note, it is an alternative for many singles and couples (either heterosexual or homosexual) who may not be able to have children due to medical, biological or physical reasons. This would impact their wellbeing emotionally, as they would have a heighted self-esteem possibly because having a child is something they have dreamt about for a long time. As this is still a controversial procedure, people choosing surrogacy may face many ethical and moral dilemmas such as what to tell the child and whether there will be contact with the surrogate mother. This would have a detrimental impact on the wellbeing of the child and surrogate mother emotionally, due to questions about sense of identity, and socially, due to gossip and prejudice.

The development of a range of emerging technologies has also impacted on health and safety. Emerging technologies such as bionic limbs give individuals who have had an amputation due to injury or disease the chance to function similarly using a prosthetic/artificial limb. This technology has a favourable impact on the individual requiring the bionic limb, as it would improve their overall wellbeing, self-esteem, sense of identity and ability to socialise and increase their physical function. A detrimental impact on the individual using this emerging technology is the access and costs associated with the procedure and prosthetic limb.

Additionally, various advancements and developments in emerging technologies have had a meaningful impact on education and learning. Emerging technologies offered through cloud computing have meant that individuals and groups can share servers, storage, documents, applications and services and collaborate on projects. This emerging technology has an impact on individuals as it leads to efficient workplace or family practices, possible decreased workload and improvements in collegiality and shared knowledge. This may enhance wellbeing socially and emotionally, as individuals feel empowered by working together and learning from each other. The wellbeing of the group/organisation may also be enhanced economically as it can save on labour and infrastructure costs, improve efficiency and manageability, and reduce maintenance. On the other hand, group wellbeing may be impacted in a negative manner as it may necessitate restructuring positions, adjusting procedures, involve high fees for charges and administration, and impact storage availability and data speed.

A selected piece of technology

Students learn about:	Students learn to:

a selected piece of technology *issues related to technological development*
• reasons for the development of the technology
• factors affecting access to and acceptance of the technology
• impact on lifestyle and wellbeing of the technology
	• conduct a case study of the selected piece of technology by considering the following questions:
	  – how has the technology emerged or developed over time?
	  – what impact has the technology had politically, economically and socially?
	  – what issues are related to the use and development of the technology?

Revision summary

There have been countless developments in technology over the past decade. **A selected piece of technology** that has had an impact on contemporary society is the smartphone. *Issues related to technological development* include **reasons for the development of the technology**, **factors affecting access to and acceptance of the technology**, and **impact on lifestyle and wellbeing of the technology**.

A smartphone is a portable, multifunctional device that has the ability to make phone calls and send messages, in addition to performing other functions. Today, these functions look very different to what they once looked like and will eventually look like in the future.

The reasons for the development of the technology known as the smartphone include its tendency to be compact, lightweight and multifunctional, as well as its portability, connectivity, functionality, durability, and cost in comparison to owning and using multiple devices.

The technology emerged and developed over time from the extension of portable (mobile) phones that simply made and received calls and text messages. In 1993, IBM produced 'Simon', which was the first production phone that people considered to be 'smart' but merely had on-the-go voice, email and fax services. Three years later, Nokia released a larger style phone capable of multi-communications called the Nokia 9000 Communicator (Pocketnow, 2014).

By 1999, Microsoft developed their version of a smartphone called a Pocket PC, with Ericsson announcing their own version of a smartphone the following year. The year 2002 made way for the Blackberry OS, which moved out of the corporate world and became accessible to mainstream users. There were a number of different smartphone releases by companies such as Nokia, Motorola, Samsung, Symbian, Palm and Microsoft during this seven-year period (Pocketnow, 2014).

In 2007, smartphones were taken to a whole new level with the introduction of the Apple iPhone and iOS. This smartphone gained huge momentum and has now become the highest revenue smartphone. Its rival, Android, was acquired by Google and in 2008 developed the HTC Dream. A couple of years later PC giant Microsoft released the Windows Phone with a lot of early promise (Pocketnow, 2014).

Since this time there has been a shift from keyboards to touch screens, and this change has seen the demise of branded smartphones from Symbian, Palm OS, Windows Mobile and BlackBerry. As a result, iOS and Android dominate the market share, with Android leading the way in volume-based market share (number of Android devices sold).

The *issues related to the use and development of the technology include* security risks and breaches, unintentional sharing of data, hacking, privacy issues, battery consumption, overheating, storage space, camera quality, vision loss, neck problems, addiction, affordability, fragility and updates.

The factors affecting access to and acceptance of the technology include:

Age and gender – children even as young as eight years old own or feel pressured to own smartphones. People of all generations and genders are accepting of technology, with adolescents and young adults tending to use their smartphones more prominently. Smartphones can be easily navigated by babies all the way through to aged individuals, and males tend to use smartphones more for gaming, while females use them for photography and social media.

Culture and religion – smartphones are used by individuals of all cultures and religions. Some cultural practices and religious beliefs might restrict the time and type of smartphone use with other cultures use functions of smartphones more prominently. Cultural and religious beliefs can be strengthened by connecting with associated members via social media; language or religious applications might make smartphones more accessible.

Education and economic status – adolescents and young adults may need access to smartphones for educational purposes while at school, university, TAFE and college. Children and adolescents attending more affluent schools may be strongly encouraged to use smartphones during lessons for classwork, and individuals from low socioeconomic families may feel the pressure to own a smartphone. Overall, smartphones are accepted by people of all educational levels and socioeconomic statuses. Individuals need to be educated about the safe use and functionality of smartphones as well as appropriate information shared about updates.

Disability and geographical location – people with disabilities and people living remotely are very accepting of smartphones as smartphones allow them to feel and be more connected. There may be applications available for people with disabilities and people living remotely; however, features may need to modified to suit the type of disability. People living in cities may feel more pressure to have the latest smartphone; there may be network connection issues for people living remotely and network traffic for people living in cities.

There has been a significant **impact on lifestyle and wellbeing**, including *politically, economically* and *socially*. Smartphones have dramatically impacted on lifestyle and wellbeing: socially – keeping individuals connected as well as capturing and storing moments; physically – tracking fitness and keeping healthy via various applications; emotionally – allowing individuals to have a positive state of mind as they feel organised; economically – storing data, keeping track of spending, accessing internet banking, working remotely; culturally – keeping track of cultural events, connecting and sharing experiences with others; spiritually – playing music, using various applications to meditate and relax and keeping individuals entertained.

Politically, smartphones have enabled countries to trade and world leaders to stay connected with each other and individuals in the countries they are serving. Smartphones have enabled instantaneous sharing of important messages and information and interactive media for political messages. Smartphones have increased people's awareness of global issues through news and social media.

Economically, smartphones have a very large market share of all technology available on the market; smartphones are a big business and have created millions of dollars for developers and owners alike. Advertisers have to fight for brand association; venue is gained in accessories; constant updates have meant individuals want the latest version; new jobs have arisen in research, development, production, selling, advertising and maintenance.

Socially, smartphones have allowed individuals to capture precious moments with family and friends; smartphones provide greater connection via numerous social media platforms. Features such as video and FaceTime have allowed individuals to interact closely, while contact lists store important personal and business information.

Use of smartphones while driving has required a variety of new laws to be legislated to keep us safe. They have streamlined the issuing of fines and demerit points for misuse.

Sample examination questions: Extended response

3   **Analyse the impact of ONE selected piece of technology on lifestyle and wellbeing.** (15 marks) (Adapted from BOS, 2012)

Smartphones are an example of a piece of technology that has a considerable impact on lifestyle and wellbeing. Lifestyle and wellbeing can be impacted in the form of health, organisation, connectedness, cultural celebration, managing finances, political matters and maintaining spirituality.

A smartphone is a mobile phone, which is a portable communication device that has numerous functions. These include making and receiving phone calls; sending and receiving a short message service (text message); sending, receiving and storing emails; taking, storing and editing photos; browsing the internet; entering events on a calendar; listening to music; and downloading various applications which have even greater functionality.

The various functions of a smartphone can be used to establish positive health decisions through tracking eating habits, logging physical activity in a calendar or using various apps to participate in physical activity and recreation such as yoga sessions. These uses impact positively on lifestyle and wellbeing, both physically and emotionally. For example, an individual may use a running application to map their route, track their pace, keep time and monitor their heart rate. They then might log this physical activity into a calendar or possibly another application alongside their meals for the day. This tracking and storing may motivate the individual and enable them to set specific fitness goals to keep them motivated, as well as empower them have a positive outlook on life.

Smartphones may also create some very unhealthy habits. Many individuals have become extremely fixated with their smartphones and do not know how to put them down. These habits have led to overuse, tension, stress, moodiness and sometimes obsessions. Couple this with research being released that individuals may be exposed to harmful radiation omitted by WiFi, this exposure and overuse could lead to possible health issues later on in life. Subsequently, all of this may negatively impact wellbeing emotionally, through anxiety, depression and isolation, and physically, due to lack of sleep, withdrawals and potential radiation exposure.

Smartphones are smart in how they have the potential to improve the planning and organisation of individuals. Individuals may use their synched and colour-coded calendar to store important meetings, dates and events; keep up to date with family/social outings and birthdays; and enter deadlines and projects for work. Setting alerts, reminders and alarms would also assist in the organisation and management of multiple role commitments. Many functions throughout a smartphone also allow for saving of important dates or events from text messages, emails and contact lists. These are also supported by applications such as notes and reminders to further enhance organisation. For example, a family may have four personal calendars that they have all synched together to assist in the family's organisation and management of responsibilities, tasks and commitments. By having them all synched, family members can arrange events, meetings and outings with these in mind. This impacts on wellbeing socially as each member can endeavour to socialise at a time that is mutually accepted and available. The consequence of this is also an improved state of mind, as they feel organised, and enables wellbeing to be enhanced emotionally.

Negative implications of this improvement in organisation are the potential for information overload and privacy to be diminished. Individuals may become so overwhelmed with all of the dates, entries and reminders that they may fail to recognise the key events in the calendar. This impacts on their wellbeing emotionally as they may become drained and anxious by all of the information shared. As long as they put a limit on either what is shared due to overload or personal privacy, individuals can continue to stay organised by using the various features offered by a smartphone.

Smartphones can also be used to establish connectedness and capture moments. By using functions such as the camera, video camera and memos, individuals can become or stay connected as well as capture and store special moments in time. Smartphones have replaced many of the digital cameras that were once used by individuals, and they have become an essential tool used as part of our lifestyle in capturing the most precious, momentous or important occasions in life such as videoing a baby's first steps or recording the opening speech given at a noteworthy work conference. Further to this is the ability of smartphones to establish greater connections to significant individuals via numerous social media platforms, through features such as video and FaceTime, and by storing important personal and business information in contacts/address books. These functions/applications have allowed individuals to interact closely and maintain a connection even if separated by distance. Subsequently, wellbeing is enhanced socially and emotionally through maintaining contact, establishing connections and enhancing self-esteem and sense of belonging amongst families and groups.

On the other hand, the use of smartphones for establishing connections and capturing moments can impact on lifestyle and wellbeing negatively. This is indicated by the breaches in privacy and safety if images are downloaded, shared and saved by strangers unknown to families and friends. Security of information can also be jeopardised by using this feature of a smartphone as, if personal or private details are shared via social media platforms or in blogs, it can put individuals at risk. This significantly impacts on wellbeing emotionally as it may lead to anxiety, depression and isolation, depending on the circumstances surrounding any potential incidents.

The use of smartphones can also impact on lifestyle and wellbeing in a cultural sense by keeping track of cultural events and celebrations through social media such as 'Events' on Facebook, establishing connections with other individuals from the same/similar culture and sharing experiences with others that may reflect similar values and beliefs. The consequence of this is that it may lead to a sense of belonging, trust and bonding. While this impacts wellbeing socially and emotionally, it can have significant impacts culturally and spiritually. On the other hand, due to differing values, opinions and beliefs, harassment and discrimination may occur, especially if cultural events, images or symbols are displayed on social media platforms such as Instagram. This would negatively impact wellbeing socially, because of possible cultural tension, and emotionally, due to lowered sense of identity or possibly doubt.

The intelligence of smartphones has enabled individuals to manage their finances more effectively through storing data, budgeting, keeping track of spending, accessing internet banking and working remotely. Lifestyle and wellbeing have changed as a result of smartphones being used for financial activity. By using applications such as banking applications, individuals can keep a close eye on their financial situation and possibly create plans and budgets for how to manage their money more effectively. This can improve wellbeing economically and emotionally as individuals feel they have some control over their money and, as a result, their self-esteem is enhanced. On the other hand, smartphones may impact individuals negatively from an economic perspective as they may spend money on updating the phone regularly, purchase unnecessary accessories, download music, use excess data, and rack up expensive phone calls. The phone may be hacked and secure information of bank and credit card details may be accessed. This would result in feelings of frustration and anger, therefore impacting wellbeing emotionally.

The use of smartphones has had an impact on political matters. Legislations have been developed by governments to keep us safe while using smartphones and to protect us as consumers. In addition, smartphones have allowed businesses and countries to trade, which can have a positive impact on wellbeing socially as well. Smartphones have also enabled individuals to stay connected with politicians and leaders via social media platforms such as Twitter, where they can clarify established policies or seek information about future directions. The announcement of important government broadcasts, political messages and global issues through news and social media has also been made possible and accessible on a smartphone. These aspects impact on lifestyle and wellbeing economically, socially and emotionally. The negative legal implications of smartphones impact wellbeing politically, physically and emotionally through the issuing of fines and demerit points for misuse and crimes associated with smartphones such as inappropriate photographs, illegal downloads, assault, robbery, and black market sales.

Therefore, it can be seen that smartphones have a considerable impact on individual, group and family lifestyle and wellbeing. Implications can be identified through health decisions, planning and organisation, establishing connectedness and capturing moments, through cultural celebrations, maintaining spirituality, attempting to manage finances, and addressing political matters.

Chapter 5

Individuals and Work

Individuals and Work is one of three options for the HSC course. Students are to study one of the three options, and it should occupy approximately 25 per cent of course time (BOS, 2013, p. 26).

Studying this option will create an understanding of why people work, the needs that it meets and how it is viewed in society. Students will gain the skills to understand statistics and current trends through learning the specific language used by the Australian Bureau of Statistics. These trends create an understanding of how work might change over the life span.

The option will show the changing nature of work as well as the influences general society has on how we perform our daily paid tasks. Students will develop and build a set of skills to combat these changes that will help to support themselves and their future lifestyles.

Understanding the structure of a workplace and entitlements will reduce the vulnerability of young people navigating into the workforce. Students will learn about the skills needed within a workplace and how to plan and prepare for a career. They will learn to maximise their employment opportunities.

It is important to note that, like in the other options, in the final examination student responses will be assessed in relation to the rubric.

The rubric is as follows:

In your answer you will be assessed on how well you:
- demonstrate knowledge and understanding of societal influences on wellbeing relevant to the question
- apply the skills of critical thinking and analysis
- communicate ideas and information using relevant examples
- present a logical and cohesive response.

HSC option: Individuals and Work

The nature of work

Students learn about:	Students learn to:
the nature of work *reasons people work* • to meet specific needs • economic • value and status	• describe how work can contribute to the satisfaction of specific needs • compare and contrast the needs that are met through paid and unpaid work • explain how values and status of work impact on how a person perceives work

Revision summary

When an individual works, they are exerting energy for a purpose. The purpose can be either paid (employed) or unpaid (domestic labour or volunteer). People choose to work for a variety of reasons. For paid workers, their motivation may be for the **economic** benefits – such as a wage or salary. It may also be for the **status** (a societal rank based on the type of employment you have) that it may gain them in the community. For those who undertake unpaid work, such as volunteers for Land Care or those on Surf Patrol at the local beach, they may work for the **value** (things that are important to the individual and/or the community) that it brings to the community or themselves, such as improving their self-esteem, supporting the environment or lending a hand to those less fortunate. Whether work is paid or unpaid will influence how **specific needs** are met. For an individual to fulfil their adequate standard of living needs, they must be in paid employment. Accessing adequate food, clothing and shelter depends on a degree of accessing finance. Whereas an individual may fulfil their sense of identity needs through both paid and unpaid work, wearing a surf lifesaving patrol uniform creates an immediate sense of belonging and ownership for a club. The same can be said for a police officer – the hours they work, the uniform they wear, the language they use, all create an understanding of who they are. Working can contribute to the **satisfaction of specific needs**. For those needs that rely on economic resources to support their satisfaction, such as adequate standard of living, only paid work will allow them to be met. For needs such as sense of identity, or even education (on-the-job learning), both paid and unpaid work can satisfy and meet those needs.

Status may influence how people *perceive* work. For those who are employed in jobs where exploitation is common and aims are less moralistic, such as the paparazzi, their employment status is not high; those jobs that are high in economic benefits or those that create protection for the community, such as firefighters, doctors and High Court judges, have a higher employment status. The decisions these individuals make and their impact on the community will influence how highly they are perceived, thus creating their status. The **value** placed on work may influence how people perceive it. For work where taxes are collected, the community perceives the work as valuable. Taxes support the community and those within it. An individual may perceive work to be of value if they are getting economic benefits, which will help support their adequate standard of living needs. An individual may also perceive work to be valuable if they gain enjoyment or a sense of purpose from it.

Sample examination questions: Short answer

1   **Describe TWO needs that are met when individuals participate in unpaid work.** (4 marks) (BOS, 2011)

Education needs: When working in unpaid employment (i.e. receiving no payment), an individual may be given the opportunity to acquire knowledge and skills, thus learn on the job. Unpaid employment can include working as an intern, on work placement or for a charity. When working in these situations, the individual will learn skills that can be transferred to paid employment. For example, if doing work placement in an industrial kitchen, the individual will learn proper work health and safety procedures, the time management of preparation and cooking meals and also communication in a stressful setting.

Health needs: While participating in unpaid work, an individual may benefit their health. This means that they can improve their physical fitness or develop their mental health while working without payment. For example, volunteer lifeguards and the State Emergency Service will increase their heart rates while working, which will ultimately improve their physical health. Those that volunteer for a charity, for example in a homelessness resource centre, can improve mental health as they can gain skills, self-confidence and self-esteem by helping others in need.

2   **Explain the significant influences on how individuals perceive work.** (6 marks) (BOS, 2013)

The value placed on work and the status of work are significant influences that will impact on how individuals perceive work. **Value** is both the personal and social worth of work. A personal will perceive their work as valuable if they receive economic benefits and if it contributes to their sense of identity. For example, consider an individual receiving payment for their role as a radio DJ; in this role they will earn money to meet their adequate standard of living needs but also be able to express themselves and develop an identity through the music they play and the conversations they have. Society will value an individual's work if it enables them to contribute back, like providing a service such as the NSW Ambulance service supporting those who are sick and injured. Society will also value work if it enables them to pay taxes and contribute to infrastructure such as roads and hospitals.

The **status** of a job can influence how individuals perceive work. Status is a societal-based rank. Society will judge work based on a number of different criteria. A job can gain status based on the level of integrity it is perceived to have; for example, a High Court judge has a higher level of integrity and therefore possibly a higher status than a tabloid journalist. The level of decision-making made on behalf of others can also influence status of work. For example, a doctor uses their knowledge to make decisions on behalf of an individual's health.

Doctors have status because they can influence the lives of society with their decisions. Society may perceive work to have a higher status based on their qualifications and the number of years they have studied. For example, it can take up to seven or eight years to become a lawyer. Based on these influences, individuals and society will make a judgement on what they perceive the status of work to be.

The labour force

Students learn about:	Students learn to:
the labour force	• research and identify current trends in the labour force in regards to age and gender
• labour force concepts and terms	
– labour force	
– employed	• account for labour force participation rates across the life span by researching:
– unemployed	
– employed part-time	
– employed full-time	– full-time versus part-time employment
– participation rate	
• labour force participation across the life span	– unemployment

Revision summary

There are common terms used to describe the workforce. The following terms are adapted from the Australian Bureau of Statistics. **Labour force:** The number of people who are working or able to work. **Employed:** An employed person is one who is aged 15 years or older who works more than one hour per week and is paid either directly or indirectly in a job, business or farm, or works one hour or more in a family business or farm without payment. Individuals are also considered employed if they were on leave, on strike or on workers' compensation. **Unemployed:** This includes anyone who is 15 years or older and is actively seeking and available for work. **Employed part-time:** Anyone working fewer than 35 hours per week. **Employed full-time:** Those working more than 35 hours per week. **Participation rate:** This is simply the labour force expressed as a percentage of the whole population.

These terms will be helpful when understanding the **current trends** in regards to the number of people working, breaking down the workforce by their **age** or **gender** and whether people work in **part-time** employment or **full-time** employment. When looking at statistics and trends it is important to see the changes to participation across our working life (the life span). The Australian Bureau of Statistics (http://www.abs.gov.au/) will enable access to current trends in the labour force in regards to age and gender, full-time and part-time participation rates and unemployment data.

Throughout the life span there will be periods of time where individuals may move between full-time work and part-time work, or periods of unemployment. Personal circumstances such as study, birth, caring for young children, family, marriage breakdown, caring for older relatives, remarriage and gender will usually dictate this. The stage at which an individual is in the life span has strong influence on the participation rate of full-time work and part-time work.

Unemployment data from the ABS shows that the unemployment rate is rising for both male and females. Unemployment is most likely to affect young workers who have only recently entered the labour force compared to middle-aged workers who have better established their skills and employment networks. For men, unemployment remains steady until their early 50s when it begins to rise and peaks at 59 years of age. For women, unemployment rates continue to decline after age 55, and this may be because women may completely leave the labour force as opposed to males who remain in the labour force and continue to seek employment. As government policy increases the retirement age, we may see the unemployment rate rise again between 60 years and 70 years due to attitudes towards older workers.

Sample examination questions: Short answer

3   **From the graph below, identify current trends and account for labour force participation for age and gender.** (6 marks)

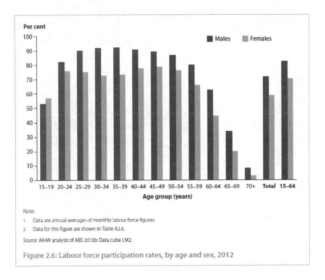

Notes

1.   Data are annual averages of monthly labour force figures.

2.   Data for this figure are shown in Table A2.6.

Source: AIHW analysis of ABS 2013b: Data cube LM2.

Figure 2.6: Labour force participation rates, by age and sex, 2012

Source: Australia's welfare, 2013. Chapter 2 Economic participation http://www.aihw.gov.au/ AIHW 2013. Australia's welfare 2013. Australia's welfare no. 11. Cat. no. AUS 174. Canberra: AIHW (accessed 12/4/16)

Age: Across the life span, age has a significant influence. We can see a sharp increase in labour force participation rates from 15–19 years to 20–24 years. This may be because young people have finished studying and are entering the workforce. For the percentage who have not worked until the end of study, their parents may have previously supported them. Between 20–24 years and 50–54 years, participation within the workforce remains relatively steady, however this only shows participation and not how many hours. It is throughout these years that an individual must work in order to support the family and meet their adequate standard of living needs. From 55–59 years to 70+ years we see a sharp decline. At this stage of the life span many are leaving the workforce altogether and retiring, or they are phasing into retirement, as you can see a small proportion still participating.

Males: Male participation differs from female participation. At 15–19 years (years of study) we see male participation to be slightly lower than females and this may be because young males have higher rates of participation in organised sport and may not have the time to gain employment while studying. From there, however, we see male participation sharply increase from 15–19 years to 20–24 years. This is the time of career establishment, networking and seeking stable employment. It then remains relatively steady until 50–54 years. Males 20–24 years and 50–54 years of age are creating financial stability, perhaps saving to afford a house, children and a comfortable retirement, which all require employment.

Females: Female participation increases rapidly from 15–19 years to 20–24 years, which, similar to males, would be the age of career establishment. In contrast to males, during a woman's 20s and 30s their participation rate drops. This drop correlates to the childbearing years of a female. During a woman's 40s her participation rate increases slightly again, which may relate to when their children are of school age. Women may re-enter the workforce with either full-time or part-time work. We also see a sharp drop in female participation from their late 50s to 70s where women may completely exit the workforce and retire.

Patterns of work

Students learn about:	Students learn to:
patterns of work • full-time, part-time, job share, casual • permanent, temporary/contract • self-employed • shift work • voluntary • seasonal • working remotely • others	• describe each work pattern and evaluate the suitability of each for different individuals across the life span

Revision summary

A *pattern of work* is simply the manner in which a particular job is worked. A pattern of work will influence the hours employed, where and what time of year the work is carried out, how stable the employment is, if an employee is entitled to benefits, the period the employee is employed for, if the work is flexible, etc. As an individual moves from their adolescent working life to having to meet the demands of a family and employer, to eventually retiring, their employment needs will differ. Therefore, some patterns of work will suit some stages of the life span more than others.

Adolescences and young adults will need flexible working patterns such as **part-time** (less than 35 hours per week plus benefits) and **casual** (paid on an hourly or daily bases with an extra loading, no benefits), as they will be trying to balance work with study such as school or university. **Shift work** (work consisting of hours outside the typical 9–5 pm) may also suit younger adults, such as those at university. Working in a bar, as a waitress in the hospitality industry, in 24-hour fast food restaurants or in retail will allow young people to study and earn a living. Other young people may work **seasonably** (work that is only available at certain times of the year), such as throughout the Christmas retail period or on the ski fields.

Adulthood is the period of life between 25 and 65 years where working patterns will change largely based on circumstances and job type. Seeking a **permanent job** for some is suitable, as they will have established job security. An individual may undertake **full-time work** (35+ hours per week plus benefits) when they are establishing a working career such as an apprentice tradesman, for example a brick layer. Once they've built their skills and become confident they may become **self-employed** (business owner/operator), creating a new business as they see a need for it. Alternatively, they may establish their career through **contract or temporary work** (an agreement for a set period of time for a set rate of pay) and move into full-time work when a position becomes available. If a woman has a child she may move from full-time work to a more flexible working pattern upon her return from parental leave. This can be as **job share** (sharing one full-time position; pay and benefits, between two people), part-time work, casually or even **working remotely** (working for a period of time away from the office, such as at home). Having the option to work flexibly allows a parent to have a greater ability to manage work and family life. Adulthood is also a time where many hours are given in a **voluntary** (offering time and performing tasks for a not-for-profit organisation) capacity. Coaching sporting teams, running the school's 'parents and friends' committee or making food drops for Meals on Wheels are all places where adults volunteer time.

The *aged* are described at those 65 years and over. At this stage of the life span, if this group haven't already retired, they may seek to phase their retirement by working casually, part-time or in a job share situation. This enables businesses to use the skills of the aged to train younger workers while only working 2–3 days per week. The cut in the number of hours worked enables this group to have time off to care for grandchildren, to rest or to pursue other interests. This may also be the time for volunteering in community organisations.

Sample examination questions: Short answer

4   **Describe ONE pattern of work and assess the suitability of it for different individuals across the life span.** (6 marks)

Voluntary work can be described as outlaying time, providing skills and giving energy for a not-for-profit business or service. Working in a voluntary capacity enables the individual to learn new skills, as most voluntary positions have on the job training schemes. These skills are invaluable, especially for adolescents and young adults trying to break into competitive careers such as radio work or as a chef. The learning of skills in an actual workplace allows the individual to gain much needed experience and to network in order to prepare and plan for a career.

Voluntary work, such as volunteering as your child's soccer coach or attending the school's 'parents and friends' meeting, can have flexible hours and can be suitable for parents who are working flexible hours in paid employment such as part-time, job share or on a temporary contract. The benefits of volunteer work and working in these areas are not only to the community but also enable busy working parents to be a strong part of their child's life and see them participate in activities where they are interacting with others and are learning new skills.

Voluntary work allows people to continue to give back to the community. For the aged, following retirement from paid work, there is a need to still feel like an active community member. Volunteering is suitable for this group to encourage a daily purpose, fulfil self-esteem and maintain a sense of identity. Volunteering at the local primary school doing the reading program or being an airport ambassador at Sydney airport will enable this group to feel a sense of worth within the community and encourage an active participation in their own lives.

Sample examination question: Extended response

1   Evaluate the suitability of THREE different patterns of work to meet the
    individual and family needs of a family consisting of two adults and two
    children aged sixteen and eleven years old. (15 marks) (BOS, 2011)

Self-employed: A self-employed worker is an owner/operator of their own
business and earns money based on the goods or service they provide. This
pattern of work may be suitable for this family, as it has the opportunity to raise
their adequate standard of living needs. A self-employed individual has total
control over their business, meaning they make all the decisions and can set the
hours worked. This may be an advantage for this family when the children have a
school event, such as a cross country run. If their father was a self-employed
plumber, he may be able to arrange appointments around the event and the
children would feel supported, creating a bond between parent and child. The
negatives of a parent being self-employed would be that in order to make a profit,
all time and energy would be put into the business, meaning family time may be
limited. During school holidays, if the second parent was working also, parents
might have to rely on the 16-year-old to care for the 11-year-old. If their children
were younger they may have to shut down the business in order to care or when
they have a family holiday, costing the business money. Ultimately, after a
business is established and becomes a reliable source of income for the family,
being self-employed can be flexible and profitable. Gaining enough time to spend
together may prove difficult during busy times (e.g. self-employed pool cleaner
over summer), thus social factors are influencing wellbeing. Individual needs will
be met, such as security and safety needs, as self-employed workers still must
maintain WHS safety procedures.

Working remotely: A remote worker is one who is working away from the home
periodically, for example, 'fly in, fly out' miners or a Navy marine on deployment.
This pattern of work may be suitable for this type of family, as there are two
adults in the family and this type of employment would not be suitable for a single
parent caring full-time. This type of work can be quite lucrative, meaning a larger
income can be earned in a short time. This can meet the family's adequate
standard of living needs by providing suitable and stable housing, food and
clothing. This may negatively influence the remote worker, such as a mother who
is in the navy and deployed for six months of the year. This may influence her
sense of identity needs as a mother, as for six months of the year she isn't seen
as a mother by those around her. Communication may also be difficult, and she
may feel like she is not fulfilling her daily roles as a mother or partner. This can
be draining and stressful on relationships, thus emotional factors are influencing
her wellbeing. This pattern of work maybe suitable for this family if the mother
was working as a news reporter, which only took her away from the family for
shorter periods. The timing and unpredictable nature of this type of job may put
more pressure on the older child, but will still allow a stronger relationship (social
factors influencing wellbeing) between mother and children.

Casual work: A casual worker is one who is employed on an hourly or daily basis,
and is paid an extra loading on top of the usual rate to make up for the lack of
usual benefits such as sick and holiday leave. This type of employment is not
particularly stable and workers may not have set hours or set days. They may be
called in on demand. For this particular family, casual work may suit the 16-year-

old child, or the 'non breadwinner' of the family. The main breadwinner of the family would need stable work, which can provide sick leave and holiday leave and pay. Casual work does not provide these benefits, which means if a child gets sick and has no other carer, the casual worker would have to miss their shift and it may go to someone who is deemed a more 'reliable' worker. This type of work would not meet the family's security and safety needs; this job type does not provide financial or job security, meaning economic factors would influence the wellbeing of the family long term. However, if the 16-year-old were to secure a casual job, individual needs such as education, employment and sense of identity could be met. Having a casual job may teach the 16-year-old time management, organisational skills, communication skills and problem-solving skills and help them to save and budget money. Acquiring these skills would increase their self-esteem, with emotional factors influencing wellbeing.

Changing work patterns

Students learn about:	Students learn to:
changing work patterns *social factors leading to changing work pattern* • employment/unemployment • perceptions of gender • family circumstances, including structural change • government policy • economics • education/retraining • technology	• analyse the relationship between patterns of work and the various social factors

Revision summary

Social factors are the changes that are happening in our contemporary society. These changes have influenced how we work. In the past we saw 9 a.m.–5 p.m. full-time, permanent jobs. However, as society adapts and changes to new laws, new technology and new attitudes to family and gender, our working lives have also adapted and changed. Many occupations that we see today were previously not in existence and, as society continues to evolve, many more occupations and working patterns will emerge. **Education** and the level of education society holds have influenced the patterns of work that we hold. Today we can see more people accessing university. There are many more colleges, institutions and online degrees that have influenced the level of study for many people. Most universities offer online options and there are many that only have online learning, opening up education to those who need flexibility, whose current situation does not allow for daily travel or those who wish to retrain. Previously, for those who left school and did not go onto further study, typically they picked up a full-time 9 a.m.–5 p.m. office jobs, starting at the bottom and hoping to earn the rights to promotion. Today with the increase in people accessing university we are seeing people needing flexible working patterns, such as part-time or casual work, to balance the demands of both work and study.

The continuing development of **technology** has created more opportunity to learn online, leading to greater employment options for the individuals who study in this manner. However, it has also been responsible for eliminating some occupations. **Robotics and automation** have supported humans to produce goods and services more efficiently and cheaply than humans producing them on their own. **Computers** running automated systems have created only the need for trained specified computer technicians in case of breakdown or fault. In the past, businesses that mass-produce products (such as the automobile industry) have needed humans to painstakingly build cars panel-by-panel, bolt-by-bolt, working 9 a.m.–5 p.m. full-time in a permanent position. Today we see the need for a limited number of workers working shift work so the automated systems can mass-produce 24 hours per day, making more to sell in a shorter and more efficient time.

Family circumstances including structural change can influence how we work. As attitudes to family change, so too does the typical family structure. Divorce, death, birth, remarriage and caring for a loved one can change our daily circumstances. The need to fulfil our adequate standard of living needs will never change, but neither will our human desire to care for and support families. Due to the costs of advertising, hiring and retraining, employers would prefer to see skilled employees return to the workplace when a family's circumstances change, for example when a baby is born. Typical, structured hours of full-time 9 a.m.– 5 p.m. positions do not allow for the flexibility of families and their needs. To entice skilled workers to return to work, employees may be offered remote work such as working from home or part-time work or even job share. This may also be a time of self-employment, using already acquired skills to create small businesses where advertising over the internet and on Facebook is cost efficient and user friendly.

Perceptions of gender relates to how we view males and females in contemporary society. Traditionally males were seen as the breadwinners and therefore worked 9 a.m.–5 p.m. full-time permanent jobs. Job security was needed but not flexibility because in a traditional family structure the female stayed at home to look after the home and the children. Today, as women are becoming more skilled and are attending university in greater numbers, they are being recognised as indispensable within the workplace. As a result, they may become the family breadwinner or, with the rise of single parenting, the only source of income for the family. Thus to fulfil both work and family roles, work has had to become flexible to accommodate their needs as well as a working mother's needs. Allowing women to work from home has enabled women to fulfil their employers' job needs while limiting travel time and working flexible hours.

Government policy relates to the laws and legislation that govern our country, and its effect on how we work. The Energy Policy of Australia has created laws to continue to support coal mining within Australia. As our natural resources are being found in further and more remote areas, we are seeing the emergence of patterns of work away from the typical 9 a.m.–5 p.m. office job. To meet our demand for coal to run our energy system, workers are flying in and flying out to remote areas where there is not enough infrastructure to support a large community. Working in relatively remote areas, employers generally provide accommodation, food and other services for workers but not for their families. Work is usually a roster with fixed days on followed by a fixed number of days off, thus workers have the time to fly home to family members.

The **economics** of Australia will be influenced by the **government policy**, as will our **employment/unemployment levels.** Our economy moves up and down, from high prosperity to extreme lows like the Global Financial Crisis. When our economy is in recession, consumer confidence is low; businesses and individuals are less likely to take risks, so there will be high unemployment. There will be less spending, less need for goods and services, and we will see a decrease in the number of small businesses opening up, thus less self-employment. Businesses will rely on contract and temporary workers and casual workers, saving much-needed funds on having to outlay benefits (sick leave and annual leave). In a boom period, there is the opposite effect: more consumer spending, more need for goods and services, thus a higher employment rate, more promotional opportunities and opportunities to bargain for flexibility in the delivery of their work.

Sample examination questions: Short answer

5   **Explain how ONE social factor may cause an individual to move from one pattern of work to another.** (4 marks) (Adapted from BOS, 2012)

Technology in the workplace, such as computers, and the advancement in telecommunications, for example the internet, have led to the globalisation of businesses. Businesses today can communicate and compete on a global scale. Because of this, jobs that were previously full-time 9 a.m.–5 p.m. (as they only competed on a national level, that is, between Australian companies) cannot be competitive with companies overseas due to time differences. We are now seeing an increase in shift work, which is when regular hours of work are based outside the standard hours. Working shift work at night in Australia allows our big businesses, for example the financial sector, to compete with companies in the northern hemisphere (UK and USA) and other financial centres such as Asia.

6   **Choose THREE of the following social factors and describe how they have led to changing work patterns.** (6 marks) (Adapted from BOS, 2011)

- **Government policy**
- **Family circumstances including structural change**
- **Perceptions of gender**
- **Education**

Government policy, such as the introduction of parental leave, has led to changing work patterns. Previously when women became pregnant and left the workplace they did not have the right to return, resulting in many women leaving their full-time employment. With the introduction of this government policy, parental leave may be taken either as a main caregiver (either male or female), as adoption leave or as leave for those in a same sex de facto relationship for up to 52 weeks, many with the right of return. This has led to work patterns changing, as the main caregiver has the right to return and may need flexible working patterns, such as job share or part-time work, to enable them to balance caring for their child and meeting the needs of the employer.

Family circumstances can include birth, death, illness or injury, or having to care for a family member. Each of these circumstances may impact on how a family meets their adequate standard of living needs through employment. In the event of the death of a main breadwinner, if in a nuclear family situation, the now sole parent may have to increase their working hours and may need to search for a stable but flexible job. Therefore, they may have to move from a contract with a defined ending or casual work where you are on-call to a permanent part-time job or a job share position. For those who worked in an office, they may seek to work remotely – within their home to help support the family and run the household while still earning income.

Education is the process of learning. Today we are seeing the subjects taught at school evolving to help combat the national skills shortage. Previously students studied subjects that provided a direct link to university entry or left school and found a low-skilled full-time job. Students can now choose subjects with practical-based learning and workplace exposure such as VET hospitality and VET construction. These subjects are taught at school and within school hours.

Students may also have access to local Technical and Vocational Education and Training (TVET) courses, which are courses taught offsite at TAFE and contribute to gaining an HSC. Many of these courses teach skills that support the service industry. The nature of this industry is based around a 24-hour service such as the hospitality, emergency plumbing or electrical services. The increase in numbers of skilled workers has expanded the service industry, thus leading to more shift workers.

Structures that support individuals in the workplace

Students learn about:	Students learn to:

structures that support individuals in the workplace
rights and responsibilities
• employees
• employers
workplace structures
• legislation, e.g. health and safety, equal employment opportunity
• work conditions, e.g. awards, grievance procedures
• trade unions
• flexible work patterns and practices, e.g. job share, flexible work arrangements
• workplace culture, e.g. childcare, prayer room, kitchen
• leave entitlements, e.g. parental, carers
	• explain the importance of rights and responsibilities in the workplace
	
	• analyse how rights and responsibilities are supported by workplace structures and affect:
	  – the wellbeing of the employer and employee in the workplace
	  – efficient work practices
	
	• examine the extent to which the workplace can provide equal access to work entitlements for females and males

Revision summary

The workplace aims to support the employee in all aspects of their working life. The government and the National Employment Standard have established a set of laws to ensure **employee's** *rights* are met. These rights relate to pay, safety, accessing grievance procedures and protection from discrimination. For a full list of rights, access the Fair Work Ombudsman website via https://www.fairwork.gov.au. When anyone is afforded rights and they take on a role within a workplace, they have *responsibilities* they must fulfil. These are the moral obligations set out by the employer to fulfil the role given to them. **Employers** have their own set of rights as well as the responsibility to ensure all employees' rights are met.

Legislation such as Health and Safety laws and Equal Employment Opportunity (EEO) laws are implemented to ensure safety and a discrimination-free workplace. These aim to increase efficiency so that a workplace is profitable. This legislation aims to reduce staff turnover through limiting workplace injury or illness. EEO aims to create an equitable and supportive working environment, ensuring there is high morale by limiting conflict and complaints.

Working conditions create clear guidelines for workers. **Awards** are a clear, industry-set document that sets out the working arrangements such as pay, leave, allowances and overtime/penalty rates. A **grievance procedure** shows a step-by-step process that employees can follow if they find them self in a dispute or conflict with another employee or their employer. These working conditions seek to ensure efficiency within the workplace. Employees will feel secure with the clear knowledge of the expectations placed upon them. They have an outlet and procedure to follow if there is conflict, reducing stress and time, thus enabling more effective problem-solving. Knowledge of leave and pay rates enables employees to budget and feel supported if they have a child, become sick or injured or need to care for a loved one.

Trade unions are organisations that were established by workers and for the workers to protect their working rights. They negotiate with employers on a collective basis, meaning that if changes were to occur that would impact on employees' rights, employees could fight together with one leader – their trade union.

Flexible work patterns and practices are arrangements made with employees to fulfil the demands of their working roles in a manner that suits them and their lifestyles. Some flexible work patterns and practices include flexible hours, working away from the office (working remotely), working part-time or job share, flexible days and flexible leave arrangements. These arrangements increase the efficiency of workers, increasing overall workplace productivity as roles and demands are met at times that suit employees, decreasing their stress and reducing staff absenteeism and turnover.

The **culture** of a workplace can either increase or decrease the desire to be productive, to attend work and even to terminate the position. Creating a workplace where employees can have open communication that is family-friendly and supportive of the diverse nature of Australian employees will create a desire to please, seek promotion, follow health and safety regulations and reduce conflict. This creates a space of higher morale and low staff turnover. Workplaces can do this by providing on-site **childcare** or pre-arranged childcare, an open and friendly **kitchen** space and a **prayer room**.

Leave entitlements are the provision of time off. **Carers** leave, **long-service** leave, **annual** leave, **parental** leave and **sick** leave enable the employer to leave the workplace to meet their needs and return at a time when they can be productive. Scheduled time off, such as annual leave, may be taken across four weeks of the year. This leave is important for the rejuvenation of employees. If off time is scheduled, employees are less likely to be absent, increasing overall productivity.

Sample examination questions: Short answer

7   **Describe how legislation contributes to efficient work practices.**
    (4 marks)

Workplace structures are crucial in a workplace environment to ensure all employees stay on task. **Legislation** is the laws that workplaces must abide by to keep the workplace safe and supportive.

Equal Employment Opportunity legislation aims to promote equality for all workers to achieve their full potential regardless of age, culture, gender, marital status or sexuality. EEO aims to eliminate discrimination when hiring, when seeking promotions and when offering retraining. This legislation ensures efficiency, as the best, most qualified worker will be working in the position. Hiring the most qualified worker will ensure they are productive (as they need less training). Eliminating discrimination at promotional levels ensures all staff will be working harder for promotion, thus increasing production and reducing staff absenteeism.

Health and Safety legislation, such as the *Work Health and Safety Act 2011*, aims to ensure the health and safety of all employees, employers and anyone who enters the workplace. This legislation creates efficiency within the workplace through the creation of clear processes and procedures for all tasks. In high-risk jobs, having a set process that is clear ensures employees remain on task, increasing their efficiency at the same task as it may be repeated regularly across the workday. For example, giving an employee training and safety equipment gives peace of mind that they will be free from risks and danger, ensuring they feel safe and supported within the workplace. This will increase morale and reduce staff turnover within the workplace, as workers are not scared to come to work.

8   **Examine the extent to which work entitlements provide equal access for females and males in the workplace.** (6 marks) (Adapted from BOS, 2012)

Regardless of gender, employees (except casual and contract workers) will have access to working **entitlements** such as carers leave, long-service leave, annual leave, parental leave and sick leave. However, despite all workplaces offering leave entitlements, accessing these entitlements may be different for males and females.

The entitlement of **long-service leave** may be accessed by an employee after a period of continuous service ranging from 7 to 15 years with the same or a related employer. Although this is available to both genders, males are more likely to access long-service leave as they are more likely to maintain continuous employment. Females may leave the labour force during childbearing years, which limits their access to this entitlement.

Carers leave is leave that all employees are entitled to take to look after a sick or injured family member. This entitlement will be largely accessible for both genders; however, workplace culture will be a strong determinant. Where a workplace is supportive and family friendly, this entitlement is accessible to both genders. For those workplaces that are not family friendly, it may be seen to question work ethic if this leave is taken. Male-dominant workplaces are usually less family friendly, limiting accessibility to the entitlement for males. For females, who generally having a more caring and nurturing nature if a child or family member becomes ill, the responsibility will usually fall on the them to provide support, increasing the need to access this type of leave.

Sick leave is leave taken by employees in order to rest and recuperate following illness or injury. This is paid time off to allow workers to make and attend doctors' appointments. To access this entitlement, suitable proof must be provided to the employer, for example, a medical certificate. A workplace that is ruled by deadlines and high productivity may discourage the use of sick days. As women are more likely to seek a doctor's opinion and retain proof of illness, they are more likely to access this entitlement. Men may be ruled by their workplace culture, limiting their accessibility to this entitlement.

Parental leave is the period of leave taken after the birth of a child (live or stillbirth), or following adoption. This leave is available to both males and females and those in a same sex de facto relationship. Both genders may access this leave, however, it is more common for the female to be the main caregiver and for them to be entitled to 52 weeks of parental leave. The female may have had a caesarean and may take longer to recuperate or she may be breastfeeding. She may even have access to workplace childcare if she returns to work. For males, there may be unspoken pressure or a workplace culture that questions masculinity, which may discourage males from taking time off after the birth or adoption of a child. Therefore, extended parental leave is seen to be available to both genders, but more accessible to females.

Sample examination questions

See Chapter 8 HSC CAFS Examination Solutions for extended response solutions.

Maintaining work and life balance

Students learn about:	Students learn to:

maintaining work and life balance
individual roles
• personal commitments and interests
  – work
  – leadership
  – parenting
  – caring
  – volunteering
  – religion
  – recreation
  – studying
  – hobbies
	• recognise that individuals may have multiple roles outside the workplace

individual strategies for managing multiple roles • negotiating and sharing roles • managing resources • using technology • accessing support • utilising workplace structures	• devise strategies that individuals can utilise to effectively manage multiple role expectations caused by changing circumstances

Revision summary

For an individual to achieve wellbeing, they must create balance in their life. This means that individuals must balance their **personal commitments** with their role/s within the workplace. For example, caring for an elderly parent or special needs dependant/s or volunteering as President of the local Little Athletics club takes extended periods of time and commitment. Some personal commitments, such as parenting, caring, volunteering and studying, require an individual to fit into other people's 'time' (such as meeting other people's deadlines, assessment/exam schedules, or medication needs), and meet other people's expectations, whereas other personal commitments can help create a life balance (recreation, hobbies, religion). For those in a leadership position, whether at work or while volunteering, there will be a greater need to implement strategies to manage these multiple roles. Leadership roles generally require more time, as a leader may need to support other people with their multiple role expectations.

There are many strategies that families can implement to effectively manage their multiple personal commitments. **Negotiating and sharing roles** requires open communication between all parties. This strategy outlines all the roles within the household. Roles are assigned to those with the skills, capabilities and resources to do them. Each person involved, for example parents, children and other family members, must have knowledge and must support the idea that they complete or fulfil that role. Rosters and calendars create a visual cue to all members and are an effective tool to implement this strategy.

Managing resources is about utilising the resources you have access to without wasting them. Once resources, both human and non-human, are recognised, it is easier to identify those resources you have surplus of and interchange those for resources you have least of. Creating a system within the household to sustain resources can mean economic resources are saved.

Using **technology** as a means of saving time and energy to be used for other multiple roles can be very effective. Using 'mechanical muscles' as opposed to using human labour can be cost and time efficient in the long term. Computers and the internet and other labour saving devices, such as kitchen appliances, vacuum cleaners or dishwashers, can free up some resources to fulfil the roles that may occur in a changing circumstance. When technology cannot be used, an individual may need to seek outside help.

Accessing support, either formally or informally, enables more human resources (perhaps at the expense of non-human-money) to be used to support the changing circumstances. Asking friends or family or seeking structured support such as a paid cleaning service means that roles that could not previously be met are fulfilled.

Sample examination questions: Short answer

9   **Describe how utilising workplace structures assists individuals in managing multiple role expectations.** (6 marks)

It can be very costly to advertise and hire new staff, so when an employee's circumstances change, the workplace has structures put in place to support the employee. Therefore, to maintain work/life balance, the individual can utilise workplace structures. The workplace aims to maintain all skilled staff where possible. When a circumstance changes, the workplace has structures such as LEAVE ENTITLEMENTS (carers, long service, annual, parental and sick leave) and FLEXIBLE WORKING PATTERNS AND PRACTICES, both of which are designed to support employees but also to reduce staff turnover and increase productivity. Leave entitlement allow a worker to take time off work, with the right of return. In many cases it is paid leave which helps ensure budgets are met and bills are paid. Working patterns that are flexible enable an individual to manage not only their workplace roles, but also other roles such as studying, caring or parenting. Choosing the days, number of days or hours that are worked allows for the increased resource of time. Time can then be used to meet the demands of other roles.

GRIEVANCE PROCEDURES and TRADE UNIONS create an outlet for employees if any disputes arise. These help create a work and life balance as disputes can be resolved quickly and efficiently, in a supportive may, increasing time for other personal commitments. LEGISLATION such as Work Health and Safety creates clear guidelines for employees and employers, which in turn increases efficiency within the workplace, again increasing the time for leisure activities or hobbies.

Sample examination question: Extended response

2   **Analyse strategies that families may use to manage the expectations of multiple roles caused by changing circumstances.** (15 marks) (Adapted from BOS, 2012)

For an individual to manage the expectation of multiple roles as well as meeting an employer's expectation effectively they will have to have strategies put in place to manage their time and resources. Changing circumstances in an individual's life will influence what strategies are used, what resources they have or the level of communication between all people involved.

Negotiating and sharing roles is a strategy that enables all invested people to have open communication about the roles they would like to take on. It may mean splitting larger roles or communicating which roles each individual would prefer. One person may have to take on more roles than others if they have the resources, such as time or money, to fulfil them. In a changing circumstance such as a mother returning to work or taking on extra study after having children she will have to negotiate and share roles within the family that previously only she took on. Older children may have to be responsible to organising younger children and their lunches, her partner may have to negotiate flexible start and finishing times so that they can pick children up from school and they may have to create a roster to divide household chores. This open communication about roles ensures everyone knows and understands their role for efficiency within the household. This will ensure emotional factors, such as stress, and social factors, such as conflict, will not influence the family group's wellbeing.

To manage resources, individuals need to recognise what resources they have and in what quantity. Recognising personal strengths (human resources, e.g. clear and concise communication) and weaknesses (impulsiveness) can also help to manage resources that individuals need to recognise the impact on management of non-human resources (such as money). The goal is to ensure that all resources are used effectively and not wasted. Some individuals may interchange their resources, and use the surplus of one resource to counteract the limited supply of another resource. For example, those in a position of leadership in paid employment, with a big deal or conference coming up, may not have **time** to clean their house, shop for food or iron their clothing. In this changing circumstance, they may use economic resources, which they are earning while working long hours. These economic resources may pay for cleaners, the extra costs of grocery delivery and/or an ironing and laundry service. When circumstances change the resource available may also change, therefore it is important to be flexible and adapt to change. This strategy may influence emotional factors by reducing stress and creating peace of mind during this extra busy period of working time, thus supporting their overall wellbeing.

Technology is adapting and changing at a fast pace. Every day new technology is available and mostly affordable to improve the work/life balance of people. Quicker communication, portable workstations, better medications, easier food preparations and robotic house appliances have helped to support people with their multiple roles, in a sense making them less laborious and perhaps quicker and easier. Using technology in parenting and caring situations limits the building and supporting of relationships, but technology can cut down the time spent on other roles such as cooking, cleaning or travel to increase the time spent on those relationships. Work roles can be made more efficient if work can be completed on laptops, smartphones or smart watches during the travel time to and from the workplace. Faster and more efficient communication networks can reduce waiting times as answers can be delivered almost instantaneously. Technology can be used effectively when circumstances change; individuals can use technology such as internet banking or online shopping if a child, partner or parent gets ill or injured, limiting their flexibility in accessing these services outside the home. For example, the internet can be used to look up recipes which will then create a shopping list that can be entered into online supermarkets. Orders can be paid securely, creating peace of mind, and then be delivered to the home at a suitable time. This will allow the individual who is caring to save much-needed energy and redirect this to the patient in need. The physical factor of saving energy will enhance the wellbeing of the carer in the changing circumstance, however the costs of technology may mean economic factors may cause ill-being.

When roles cannot be managed, an individual with multiple roles may access support. This means to seek help from those around you, which may be either formal or informal. Formal support such as a structured businesses or charities can provide either paid or unpaid services. Informal support means accessing the use of friends, family or others close to you. In changing circumstances, individuals may need to access extra help to maintain a work and life balance. When work meetings run expectantly over time a parent can access a friend or family member to pick their child up from school. If the meeting structure was to change within the workplace, the parent may utilise the formal support of after-school care. By accessing these supports the parent can concentrate on their employer's needs within the meeting and have the knowledge that their child is safe in a supportive environment. These feelings (emotional factors) will influence the parent's overall wellbeing.

At any one time, depending on the circumstance, all strategies can be used independently or in conjunction with each other.

Youth employment

Students learn about:	Students learn to:

youth employment
issues that impact on youth employment
• personal management skills required in the workplace
• steps taken to prepare and plan for a career
• predominant patterns of work of young people
• rights and responsibilities of young people in the workplace
	• conduct a case study of the issues that impact on youth employment by considering the following questions:
	  – what are the factors contributing to youth unemployment?
	  – how can a young person optimise their employment prospects?
	  – how does work support young people to manage multiple roles?

Revision summary

Youth are considered to be between the ages of 14 and 24 years of age. This time of the life span is characterised by significant growth and development. The brain is also processing and strengthening at this time and, because of this, youth can be considered vulnerable. This is especially in the workplace, as the part of the brain that develops last is the part responsible for the ability to problem solve, plan ahead, think about consequences of actions, and control impulses.

Until the brain is fully developed, decision-making may rely on the part of the brain that is also associated with emotions, aggression and impulsive behaviour. This alone puts youth at risk of exploitation and workplace injury.

As a young person just starting out, their lack of skills and knowledge and their developing brains make it difficult to gain employment. It is for these reasons that developing **personal management skills** is important. The ability to plan, organise, have clear communication, make rational decisions and problem solve is essential for an employee to be reliable in the workplace. A young person can develop these skills through involvement in extracurricular activities, such as debating, sporting teams, volunteering through charities or organisations such as the St John's first aid. Businesses need their employees to be productive and efficient in order to be successful in a competitive market; developing these personal management skills will optimise their employment prospects. While at school, a young person can take **steps to prepare and plan for their career**.

Many schools have access to VET (Vocational Education and Training) and TVET (Technical and Vocational Education and Training) courses. These courses enable students to study and complete all or part of a nationally recognised qualification either at a TAFE during school hours or at school. Each VET or TVET course has either a strongly recommended or compulsory practical workplace component within community workplaces. These link students to

employers, enabling students to gain hands-on skills and training and meet with possible future employers. Students wanting to plan and prepare for their career should often do work experience in that area. This will enable them to gain skills and seek out information about the career, such as working hours, average wages/salary, working patterns available, and specialised skills needed.
Predominant work patterns of young people will revolve around supporting them to manage work and study. While studying to build a career, many young people access casual and part-time work to support themselves financially. Within the workplace, all young people have the same **rights and responsibilities**; however, as young people are more vulnerable to exploitation it is important that they have the knowledge of their rights.

Sample examination questions: Short answer

10   Describe TWO rights and responsibilities of young people within the workforce. (4 marks)

Young people have exactly the same rights (entitlements) and responsibilities (moral obligations) as other employees. However, due to their inexperience within the workplace, young people are more vulnerable to exploitation and are less likely to speak up for fear of losing their job.

Young people have the right to a working environment that is free from discrimination. They are protected under the *Anti-discrimination Act 2011* and from unfair dismissal. Having access to this entitlement means that young people have the moral obligation to ensure that they do not discriminate or vilify other employees, employers or customers/clients.

Young people are also vulnerable to workplace injuries. Along with all other employees and employers, they have the right to a safe working environment under the Work Health and Safety Act. This right ensures that young people have access to safety procedures and equipment that will minimise or eliminate harm. All workers, including young people, will have the moral obligation to follow all safety procedures, use all safety equipment, and alert their employers if there is a breech.

11   Describe the factors contributing to youth unemployment and how a young person can optimise their employment prospects. (6 marks)

Youth unemployment can happen for young people after studying in areas where there is little to no employment prospects. For example, studying for four years at university for jobs such as radio and television presenters may lead to unemployment. Understanding the job market and choosing to study in areas where there is a high demand will increase the opportunity to gain employment.

A lack of experience and hands on training can also be a problem. Young people do not yet have the experience within a workplace that older workers have. Without skills and workplace-specific training, young people can be difficult to employ. Despite study, employers are now seeking experienced employees. In order to increase job prospects, young people need to undertake areas of study that have regular and recognised workplace training attached. Entering into a workplace and meeting employers and other employees enables a young person to network and display the skills that they have. This ensures an opportunity to show initiative and work ethic to potential employers. Seeking extra volunteer work within an industry also shows an employer a strong desire to work and to learn.

Youth unemployment is also rising due to technology. Technology has decreased the number of low-skilled jobs, so occupations that young people could have previously taken and entered into the workforce to gain 'workplace skills' are no longer available or are in less demand. For example, retail shopping and the need for retail assistants, a common occupation for young people, has decreased as now a larger proportion of shopping goes online. Automated machines that customers can use to put sales through themselves if they go into a store now replace retail assistants. To maximise employment prospects, young people now have to use learn and use technology to become more marketable to employers.

Chapter 6

Multiple-choice Solutions

Chapter 1 – Research Methodology

Question	Answer
1	C
2	D
3	D
4	D
5	D
6	D
7	B
8	C
9	D
10	B
11	B
12	D
13	A
14	B
15	C
16	B
17	C
18	C
19	D
20	D
21	C
22	B
23	B
24	D
25	C
26	C
27	D
28	D
29	C
30	B

Chapter 2 – Groups in Context

Question	Answer
1	C
2	B
3	C
4	D
5	B
6	B
7	D
8	C
9	A
10	D

Chapter 3 – Parenting and Caring

Question	Answer
1	B
2	B
3	B
4	C
5	C
6	A
7	B
8	A
9	D
10	C
11	A
12	B
13	D
14	B
15	D
16	A
17	A
18	A

Chapter 7

HSC CAFS Examination 2015

Section I – 75 marks

Part A – 20 marks
Attempt Questions 1–20
Allow about 35 minutes for this part

Use the multiple-choice answer sheet for Questions 1–20.

1 Which of the following is a form of secondary data?
(A) Case studies
(B) Government websites
(C) Interviews
(D) Observations

2 What is the main cause of homelessness for women?
(A) Mental illness
(B) Domestic violence
(C) Lack of education
(D) Financial difficulties

3 Which of the following names TWO government agencies that provide support to young parents?
(A) Respite care and Carers NSW
(B) Transition Care Programs and Schools
(C) Family and Community Services and Centrelink
(D) Childcare services and Home and Community Care Program

4 Which of the following is a community organisation?
(A) Medicare
(B) Centrelink
(C) NSW Health
(D) Meals on Wheels

5 Parents Without Partners NSW Inc is an organisation that aims to create opportunities for sole parents to meet people and make friends. What is such an organisation trying to achieve?
(A) Ensuring equity for sole parents
(B) Providing education for the community
(C) Improving the wellbeing of its members
(D) Promoting understanding of legislation

6 What is one advantage of using data from digital sources in research?
(A) Equity of access
(B) Ease of searching
(C) Reliability of the data
(D) Accuracy of the source

7   What is the purpose of research?
(A) To increase understanding
(B) To ensure ethical behaviour
(C) To make use of questionnaires
(D) To formulate a research proposal

8   How can the long-term needs of the homeless best be met?
(A) By increasing public awareness
(B) By promoting the group's rights
(C) By increasing crisis accommodation
(D) By providing access to support programs

9   Biological parents are defined as individuals who
(A) are unable to adopt children.
(B) provide respite care for children.
(C) provide genetic material to create a baby.
(D) give birth to a child who differs from them genetically.

10   Why is it important to develop a timeline when conducting a research study?
(A) To manage resources
(B) To assess the data collected
(C) To reflect on problems encountered
(D) To clearly document the research proposal

11   Paul is visually impaired and supports his family through his employment in aged care. Which need is currently being met for Paul and his family?
(A) Health
(B) Education
(C) Sense of identity
(D) An adequate standard of living

12   When parents adopt a democratic style of parenting, they
(A) make supportive decisions.
(B) become the only decision makers.
(C) have little commitment to family responsibilities.
(D) do not provide any boundaries or responsibilities.

13   Which of the following can help to increase the validity of results in a research study?
(A) Relying on personal judgement
(B) Using only one research method in data collection
(C) Collecting primary data before collecting secondary data
(D) Investigating secondary sources to gain background knowledge

14   Which combination of factors has the greatest effect on homeless people and their access to services?
(A) Level of education and age
(B) Gender and social identity
(C) Employment and personal issues
(D) Socioeconomic status and culture

15 Which of the following is an example of financial preparation for parenting?
(A) Participating in prenatal classes
(B) Organising parental leave options
(C) Purchasing child safety equipment
(D) Subscribing to parenting magazines

16 Which of the following is most important when formulating research conclusions?
(A) Summarising the data
(B) Protecting the sources of data
(C) Drawing findings from sampling methods
(D) Comparing key findings between primary and secondary data

17 Which of the following best describes respite care?
(A) A community nurse prescribes medication.
(B) Modifications are made to the physical environment.
(C) The primary carer is given temporary relief from their caring duties.
(D) A health case worker from the local hospital makes weekly visits to the home.

18 Which of the following is an example of duty of care?
(A) Providing positive role models
(B) Supervising children in a playground
(C) Praising a child for achievements at school
(D) Encouraging children to participate in household tasks

19 Which of the following is most important when formulating a research proposal?
(A) Forming a hypothesis as a question
(B) Ensuring the area of study is manageable
(C) Gathering a variety of background print sources
(D) Choosing appropriate participants for primary research

20 Which of the following provides financial support to people with a short-term disability?
(A) Sickness allowance
(B) Unemployment benefits
(C) Disability Support Pension
(D) Child Disability Assistance Payments

Part B – 55 marks
Attempt Questions 21–28
Allow about 1 hour and 40 minutes for this part

NOTE: In the examination, answer the questions in the spaces provided. These spaces provide guidance for the expected length of response. If you run out of lines, ask for another booklet and continue writing.

Question 21 (10 marks)
(a) Explain how sampling contributes to reliable and valid research. (4 marks)

(b) Propose strategies which could be used to ensure that individuals involved in a research study are shown respect and privacy. (6 marks)

Question 22 (6 marks)
Examine how access to childcare services affects the wellbeing of first-time parents.

Question 23 (8 marks)
A student plans to conduct a research project on the impact of social media on youth.

Assess the suitability of using BOTH a questionnaire AND a case study as research methods for this topic.

Question 24 (8 marks)
John has just completed university. His mother has recently been involved in a major car accident. John is now required to provide full-time care for his mother.

Explain the preparations John could undertake as a carer to ensure his mother's wellbeing.

Question 25 (3 marks)
Explain how the characteristics of people with disabilities may affect their access to services.

Question 26 (4 marks)
How can informal support assist parents to fulfil their parental responsibilities?

Question 27 (8 marks)
Answer the following question in relation to ONE of the groups listed below:
  • Aged
  • Culturally and linguistically diverse communities
  • Aboriginal and Torres Strait Islander peoples
  • Rural and remote families
  • Gay, lesbian, bisexual, transgender, intersex communities
  • Sole parents
  • Youth.

To what extent have attempts to improve community attitudes towards the group affected its wellbeing?

Question 28 (8 marks)
Answer the following question in relation to ONE of the groups listed below.
The group you select can be the same as or different from the group you used in Question 27:
  • Aged
  • Culturally and linguistically diverse communities
  • Aboriginal and Torres Strait Islander peoples
  • Rural and remote families
  • Gay, lesbian, bisexual, transgender, intersex communities
  • Sole parents
  • Youth.

How have government policy and legislation helped the group to achieve equity within the wider community?

Section II – 25 marks

Attempt ONE question from Questions 29–31
Allow about 45 minutes for this section

Answer parts (a) and (b) of the question in a writing booklet Answer part (c) of the question in a SEPARATE writing booklet.

Your answers will be assessed on how well you:
- demonstrate knowledge and understanding of societal influences on wellbeing relevant to the question
- apply the skills of critical thinking and analysis
- communicate ideas and information using relevant examples
- present a logical and cohesive response

Question 29 – Family and Societal Interactions (25 marks)
Answer parts (a) and (b) of the question in a writing booklet.
(a) Outline how individuals in society are protected by legislation. (4 marks)

(b) How does current legislation support access to assisted reproductive technology? (6 marks)

Answer part (c) of the question in a SEPARATE writing booklet.
(c) Assess the effectiveness of child protection and safety legislation in supporting the welfare of children. (15 marks)

OR

Question 30 – Social Impact of Technology (25 marks)
Answer parts (a) and (b) of the question in a writing booklet.
(a) Outline the economic benefits, for individuals, which result from the development of technology. (4 marks)

(b) How can age and education affect an individual's access to and acceptance of technology? (6 marks)

Answer part (c) of the question in a SEPARATE writing booklet.
(c) Assess the possible impact of technology on interpersonal relationships within families. (15 marks)

OR

Question 31 – Individuals and Work (25 marks)
Answer parts (a) and (b) of the question in a writing booklet.
(a) Outline the personal management skills required by youth in the workplace. (4 marks)

(b) How does labour force participation vary across the life span? (6 marks)

Answer part (c) of the question in a SEPARATE writing booklet.
(c) Assess how employees' rights and responsibilities are supported by workplace structures. (15 marks)

Chapter 8

HSC CAFS Examination 2015 Solutions

This chapter contains suggested answers to the 2015 HSC CAFS Examination paper. Throughout the answers we have used a simple code to demonstrate how student answers need to use language that relates directly to the Glossary of Key Words, the knowledge and content related to the syllabus, and how the knowledge and content is used to answer the question specifically.

For example, when the text is **BOLD AND ITALICS, these words/phrases relate directly to the glossary word.** When words, phrases and sentences are underlined, they relate directly to syllabus terminology. This shows your understanding of the content and usually contains characteristics and features. When words, phrases and sentences are shaded, they relate directly to what the question is asking and indicate that you must make connections between the syllabus content and what the question is asking you.

Section I, Part A

Multiple-choice answer key

Question	Answer
1	B
2	B
3	C
4	D
5	C
6	B
7	A
8	D
9	C
10	A
11	D
12	A
13	D
14	A
15	B
16	D
17	C
18	B
19	B
20	A

Section I, Part B

Question 21 (10 marks)
(a) Explain how sampling contributes to reliable and valid research.
(4 marks)

Sampling has a *significant effect* on the reliability and validity of research. Sampling can *effectively* contribute to valid research. Validity refers to the accuracy of the data obtained. Research is valid if it accurately reflects what it was intended to measure. By choosing samples that are representative of the population and specific to the research, the data will consequently be enhanced and accurate. For example, if the research aims to accurately study youth, then the sample group must only contain people 15–24 years of age.

Reliability refers to the consistency of measurement. If research were to be conducted again under similar conditions, similar results would present. Reliability *can be enhanced* by using an appropriate research method, choosing an appropriate sample group *by using a method* such as random sampling, selecting a large sample size to be representative of the population. For example, when a large group is sampled (from all SES, genders, ages and a variety of cultural groups, compared to just using family and friends), there will be a larger variety of views, opinions and thoughts, thus increasing the likelihood of similar results if the methodology tool were to be used again under similar conditions.

(b) Propose strategies which could be used to ensure that individuals involved in a research study are shown respect and privacy. (6 marks)

It is *essential* to ensure individuals involved in a research study are shown respect and privacy. This can be done before, during and after primary research is conducted.

One such strategy to show respect is to seek permission from an individual involved in a research study before the commencement of conducting primary research through methods such as questionnaires, interviews and observations. The purpose and intentions of the research study need to be made clear through constant communication with the individual being researched, as this ensures respect. *This could be done* by seeking consent and signed documentation by the individual or guardian/s of the individual involved in the research as well as seeking permission when recording devices are used.

Another strategy to ensure respect is to *ensure* the safety, feelings and needs of the individual involved in research are maintained throughout. Voluntary involvement and request to withdraw at any time are rights of the individuals involved in research which demonstrate respect and privacy. The careful wording of questions; the avoidance of questions sensitive or offensive in nature; and maintaining respect in terms of culture, religious values and beliefs, gender, sexual and disability are all important. *This could be done* through careful planning and organising by the researcher as well as adopting ethical behaviours such as integrity for the subject to ensure respect and privacy.

The strategy of avoiding certain questions that are too private or reveal specific details about the individual being researched is important to adopt to ensure privacy of the individuals involved in a research study. The secure storage of results and data and subsequent shredding prior to disposal *could also be adopted* to ensure privacy.

Requesting anonymity could also be *another strategy adopted* by the researcher to uphold privacy. When subjects involved in research put a name to questionnaires, the inclusion of their name may result in researcher bias and as a result lead to unreliable and invalid results. *By using non-identifying codes* such as letters, numbers or codes and not disclosing the names of the subjects involved in the research, respect and privacy are maintained.

Question 22 (6 marks)
Examine how access to childcare services affects the wellbeing of first-time parents.

Child care services are a formal support. When a first-time parent accesses childcare, they are finding a placement for their young child to be cared for by trained professionals. Accessing a childcare centre will affect the wellbeing of parents *differently, depending on their circumstances*.

Placing a firstborn child into an unknown situation will be difficult for a first-time parent, as might finding the right place for the child that the parents can trust. Accessing childcare placements can be extremely difficult, which may mean parents, if desperate for the placement, may have to compromise on the service. For example, accepting a placement at a big centre as opposed to a small family day care centre. *This may create* feelings of anxiety and stress and may lead to conflict about whether or not to return to work, thus emotional factors will influence wellbeing. However, *it's important to note that* emotional factors will lead to the satisfaction of wellbeing; parents will have peace of mind with the knowledge that their child is safe (childcare services follow strict rules) and looked after by loving and trained professionals.

Economic factors will influence the wellbeing of a first-time parent. As they are a first-time parent they may be returning to work because they cannot afford to maintain their adequate standard of living needs without the income. Using a childcare centre *as opposed to* informal supports like grandparents will affect wellbeing economically. Child care services are expensive, and despite the government rebate, some first-time parents will return to work just to pay for childcare. *For those who are* economically stable, using childcare services, *although difficult* for a parent, might be a necessary way for their 'only' child to socialise and interact with other young children. This might influence emotional factors for the mother as they feel they are doing their best for their child to adapt to social norms. First-time mothers may also enjoy some time away from the dependant and may use it to socialise (social factors) or go to the gym (physical factors).

Question 23 (8 marks)
A student plans to conduct a research project on the impact of social media on youth.

Assess the suitability of using BOTH a questionnaire AND a case study as research methods for this topic.

Questionnaires and case studies *can be suitable* methods of research to conduct a research project on the impact of social media on youth, **but there may be some limitations**. Both of these types of methodologies collect primary data, which can be used to analyse and draw conclusions on the impact of social media on youth.

Case studies are a detailed investigation on a particular focus area, issue, individual, group or organisation conducted over a period of time, potentially as long as weeks, months or years. As case studies show a process or how a change has occurred, *it may be a suitable method to conduct research on* the topic of the impact of social media on youth. Case studies use a variety of research methods, such as questionnaires, interviews observations and literature reviews, to collect the large amounts of data needed to ensure a case study is reliable and the results are valid. However, using all of these methods may become too confusing for a student to create the tools and to go out and collect the data, *making the case study a difficult methodology to conduct.* However, if the student is supported to create the tools and given time to collect the data, *BOTH the case study and the questionnaire are suitable methods to use in conjunction with each other.* As a case study is conducted over a large period of time, the impact of social media on youth may not be fully realised in the youth stage of the life span and significant effects may not be evident until later in adult life. *Thus a case study may prove to be an unsuitable method of research for this topic.*

The suitability of using a case study for this topic of research *may also be questioned* due to the fact that case studies can be subjective and researchers may find it difficult not to become involved and thus negatively influence the results for this topic and the reliability of the results. As a questionnaire is largely quantitative data and the detailed data collection from a case study is qualitative, the data from both methods can be collated and compared to *help support valid and reliable conclusions* on this topic.

A questionnaire *is a suitable methodology* for the topic on the impact of social media on youth. This methodology collects primary data that can be both quantitative and qualitative data through the use of open and closed questions. Data that is obtained will reflect the thoughts, feelings and ideas related to the topic of the impact of social media on youth, such as how often do you use social media, and have you ever felt unsafe using social media. The sample group of youth will also *respond more positively* to the shorter and quicker data collection method of a questionnaire as opposed to a case study. The presentation, distribution and data collection can be done through a number of different means.

This type of research method *may also be effectively* used to distribute questions via a suitable sampling method, such as stratified sampling, to gain a large range of samples from the sample group. This may *increase the reliability of the research*, as it is representative of the population or those who may be able to comment on the impact of youth. In addition, parents, teachers, peers and friends can also have an opportunity to share their thoughts about the impact of social media on youth, making questionnaires *a highly suitable research method* to conduct research on this topic, although the detail provided in a questionnaire *may be limited.*

Question 24 (8 marks)
John has just completed university. His mother has recently been involved in a major car accident. John is now required to provide full-time care for his mother.

Explain the preparations John could undertake as a carer to ensure his mother's wellbeing.

The preparations John has to undertake as a carer to ensure his mother's wellbeing include changing health behaviours, organising finances, modifying the physical environment and enhancing knowledge and skills.

Through changing health behaviours, John has to consider his nutritional needs and eat fresh foods and drink plenty of water to cope with the physical demands of caring for his mother and to maintain energy throughout his day. John *could also engage* in regular group physical activity with or without his mother to improve his physical fitness and capacity in case he has to lift, move or transport his mother because of her inability to do so. This could be supported by spiritual connections incorporated into art forms such as yoga or Tai Chi or possibly stress management strategies such as deep breathing. These **strategies would support his mother's wellbeing, as the more he is connected to his role, the more supportive he will be to his mother. This is because caring can be draining and overwhelming**.

By modifying the physical environment, John needs to consider housing, amenities and equipment to ensure his mother's **physical and emotional wellbeing**. If his house is an inappropriate space for his mother to stay, John may need to look at buying or renting something more suitable. *He also needs to* ensure that entries and exits into the house are safe for his mother by installing ramps or non-slip surfaces. Bathrooms could have rails in the shower and toilet, a raised toilet seat, low temperature tap ware and non-slip flooring. Equipment obtained by John to support his mother may include electric beds, wheelchairs or any other modified household appliances *to better support her* physical wellbeing and ensure she is safe and comfortable.

John *could also prepare* by enhancing his knowledge and skills through enrolling in a community college carer course or any other support service that offers education and training *to better support* his mother's physical wellbeing. John could also access information from community services such as People with Disability or seek more information about her condition via the internet on reputable and reliable sites such as Care Aware. John *could also* work on his skills by *liaising with a community nurse or hospital* to show him how to care for his mother to better support her physical and emotional wellbeing.

By also organising finances, John *can ensure* his mother's economic and emotional wellbeing is further supported. Researching support payments through Centrelink, seeking advice from a financial advisor and budgeting *can help* support John's mother's economic wellbeing. This *needs to be done* to pay for their housing expenses, home modifications, medications, specialised care and even John's accumulated university expenses. Knowing they are financially stable would prove comforting for her, thus improving her emotional wellbeing.

Question 25 (3 marks)
Explain how the characteristics of people with disabilities may affect their access to services.

The characteristics of people with disabilities such as first language spoken, culture, type of disability, age, gender, level of education and socioeconomic status may affect their use of the services available to them.

First language spoken and culture *may affect* a person with a disability *in terms of* limiting their ability to understand key information about the service due to language or cultural barriers (genders mixing in a hydrotherapy pool will restrict some cultural groups). The type of disability and age *may affect* what sort of services they can possibly access due to physical (e.g. access a building without ramps) or age restrictions.

Level of education and socioeconomic status *may affect* the access of a person with a disability if they do not have an understanding of the available services. A low socioeconomic status *may mean that* they do not have access to a computer or smartphone, thus inhibiting their access to services offered on the internet through online groups or the advertisement of physical support services in the community.

Question 26 (4 marks)
How can informal support assist parents to fulfil their parental responsibilities?

Informal support such as relatives, friends and neighbours can assist parents to fulfil their parental responsibilities of duty of care, setting limits and discipline. Informal support can assist parents in their responsibility of duty of care *by providing* for the needs of the child. When parents leave children with informal supports, duty of care is assumed by the person who takes care of the child. For example, grandparents would have a duty of care to keep the children safe, fed, clothed and bathed while the parents are at work.

Informal support can assist parents *in* setting similar limits to what is expected by providing rules and boundaries to ensure that children are safe and secure. Friends *can* set limits with children around playing or interacting with other children to ensure they socialise in a fun and exciting way while being safe.

Discipline also supports the wellbeing, needs and safety of children. Parents *may need to ask* neighbours (those that live around them) to disciple their children while they are out at an appointment or at home doing other household tasks. Neighbours may need to reprimand children to fulfil the duty of care of keeping the children safe.

Question 27 (8 marks)

Answer the following question in relation to ONE of the groups listed below:

- **Aged**
- **Culturally and linguistically diverse communities**
- **Aboriginal and Torres Strait Islander peoples**
- **Rural and remote families**
- **Gay, lesbian, bisexual, transgender, intersex communities**
- **Sole parents**
- **Youth.**

To what extent have attempts to improve community attitudes towards the group affected its wellbeing?

Group: Aged

The aged are those individuals who are aged 65 years and over. They are often seen within the community as 'bad drivers', 'too slow', 'not useful', 'grumpy old men' and 'past their used by date'. The group has attempted to improve community attitudes towards the group through a number of different ways, and this in turn has positively influenced their wellbeing, helping them reintegrate back into society and become contributing members.

Recognising grandparents on Grandparents Day, a strategy implemented by the Council on the Ageing to improve community attitudes, has supported the satisfaction of wellbeing for this group. Grandparents Day is a nationwide initiative that aims to connect or reconnect grandparents to children by inviting grandparents to share a day within schools. *The aim is* for younger generations to view the aged as active members who can pass advice from one generation to the next. Grandparents Day *is successful,* as grandparents are able to show their skills and give their knowledge, or share stories from the past, as it validates their existence. The confidence and pride resulting from this day will influence the emotional factors associated with satisfying wellbeing. Increasing contact with younger generations can influence social factors of wellbeing by creating stronger relationships. *However,* each individual aged person can only experience these feelings if they are involved in Grandparents Day, they are a grandparent (which some aged people are not), and if the school supports this.

The local Men's Shed Association is a community initiative that enables older men to come to a central place in the local community and use the skills they have developed over their working life. This movement has opened up its target group from just men following retirement to all males aged 6–96 years. *While this is not a national initiative to improve community attitudes*, increasing the age range to allow all ages into workshops encourages the interaction between older generations and younger generations. It is a place to bond over the learning of skills in a language that men can understand, *resulting in a change* in community attitudes towards the group *on an individual level*, which may have *longer lasting effects* than other initiatives. When males who in their workplace had power and status eventually leave the workplace, they may lose a sense of identity, feel as though their skills are no longer useful and lose confidence in their abilities. One-on-one contact with someone who can listen and learn while making goods for the community *will promote* the wellbeing of those men. Wellbeing is enhanced socially by communicating with others, learning from young people and forming a bond, emotionally, as they can feel a sense of pride in knowing they can still achieve something, and spiritually, as they regain a sense of belief in themselves.

Question 28 (8 marks)
Answer the following question in relation to ONE of the groups listed below.
The group you select can be the same as or different from the group you used in Question 27:
   • **Aged**
   • **Culturally and linguistically diverse communities**
   • **Aboriginal and Torres Strait Islander peoples**
   • **Rural and remote families**
   • **Gay, lesbian, bisexual, transgender, intersex communities**
   • **Sole parents**
   • **Youth.**

How have government policy and legislation helped the group to achieve equity within the wider community?

Group: Youth

Youth are considered to be individuals who are between the age of 15 and 24 years. It is a time where they are finishing school and beginning to establish a career. Physiologically, the brain is not yet from fully developed. The section of the brain relating to decision-making is the last to fully develop and does not do so until their early twenties. It is for this reason that government policy and legislation has been implemented to ensure youth are not exploited and that there is equality between this group and the wider community.

The *Young Offenders Act 1997* gives those in authority the option of giving warnings and cautions to young people suspected of committing an offence. This means that young people may not have to go to court or have a conviction recorded – essentially giving them a second chance. **The effect of this** Act is that it creates equality for young people as it recognises that poor decisions can be made as a result of peer pressure, drugs or alcohol or inexperienced brain development. It recognises the need for consequences without a lifetime impact and that young people can be rehabilitated without the harsh penalties given to an adult.

The Crimes Act dictates the age of consent (16 years in NSW, QLD, VIC, WA and 17 years in SA and TAS). The age of consent laws are designed to protect children and young people from sexual exploitation and abuse. These laws determine that children and young people do not have the emotional maturity to consent to sexual activities. *The implementation of this Act leads to* equality between youth and the wider community by ensuring that this group are not engaging in sexual behaviour until they have the psychological capacity to give consent and the emotional maturity to recognise the consequences of such behaviour for themselves and their future.

The *Liquor Act 2007* makes it illegal to consume and purchase alcohol under the age of 18 years. This law does not cover parents providing alcohol to young people in their own home. *This law is the result of recognising* that young people do not have the physical capacity or the mental capacity to deal with the effects of alcohol. This Act ensures equity as it aims to keep youth safe from the negative consequences of alcohol use. However, it also ensures equity by recognising that young people in the company of parents may access alcohol (for perhaps cultural or religious purposes), so that in a controlled environment, with mature adults, they may lessen the risks.

Each of these legislations has been implemented to ensure youth have the right to a safe and healthy life.

Section II – 25 marks

Attempt ONE question from Questions 29–31
Allow about 45 minutes for this section

Answer parts (a) and (b) of the question in a writing booklet Answer part (c) of the question in a SEPARATE writing booklet.

Your answers will be assessed on how well you:
- demonstrate knowledge and understanding of societal influences on wellbeing relevant to the question
- apply the skills of critical thinking and analysis
- communicate ideas and information using relevant examples
- present a logical and cohesive response

NOTE: **Question 29 – Family and Societal Interactions – is not covered in this text.**

Question 30 – Social Impact of Technology (25 marks)

(a) Outline the economic benefits, for individuals, which result from the development of technology. (4 marks)

There are *various economic benefits* for individuals that result from the development of technology. Within the development of communication technology, consumers *benefit economically* in that mobile phones developers are constantly looking at ways to use recycled materials and make the phone more multi-functional, while phone companies are constantly creating very competitive mobile phone packages.

These economic benefits are also afforded to transport. The research and development of electric cars has given rise to low maintenance, improved fuel efficiency, better fuel consumption and financial incentives for purchasing electric cars. These features not only **benefit the individual financially, but also can lead to economic benefits** for the community *as well reducing* the economic impact of greenhouse gases resulting from petrol-fuelled cars.

Consumer services such as those offered online both nationally and internationally have had a considerable economic impact on individuals. The development of this online technological support has *meant* that individuals can seek help, advice and guidance through the use of products and services. Blogs, YouTube clips and online support have meant that instead of calling a home handyman or being charged by the hour by a supplier, consumers can use do-it-yourself videos and information to maintain or use technology such as smart washing machines.

(b) How can age and education affect an individual's access to and acceptance of technology? (6 marks)

Age is a significant reason for why the access and acceptance of technology varies. Generational differences are shaped by exposure and use of technology throughout the life span. In today's society, children and youths are exposed to a whole range of technology from a young age in their school and family life. *This may result* in greater acceptance and openness to the use of new technologies and **may result** in more regular experimentation, **whereas** some adults and aged individuals may lack the knowledge of different technologies, therefore *contributing to negativity and a reluctance* to use new technology. For example, aged individuals may fear online banking due to their lack of exposure and knowledge of the service. Adolescents may be already using the service as they have become comfortable using it and are not fearful of the technology.

Access and acceptance of technology also varies due to education. An individual's level and educational status or skills they have developed using technology can *contribute* to the type of technology they have access to. If a child or youth does not have regular use of technology at school, it may create a *negative effect* on their ability to use technology later on in life, such as in the workforce. This may then *affect further acceptance* of new technology due to their lack of use. If individuals have a *positive experience* with technology, such as those enrolled in distance education, then it *gives rise to ease of use* of other forms of technology.

(c) Assess the possible impact of technology on interpersonal relationships within families. (15 marks)

Technology has a *significant impact* on interpersonal relationships within families. *This is evident* with household technology, entertainment technology and information and communication technology. Household technology *impacts* interpersonal relationships through saving time and money as well as possible reliance on the technology. Information and communication technology can assist families to capture memories and stay connected, but may lead to unhealthy technology habits such as too much screen time. Lastly, entertainment technology can bring families closer together or tear them apart through overuse.

Household technology has come a long way from primitive examples such as washboards and cast iron kettles to complex household technology examples such as dual washer/dryers and professional electric coffee machines. Today, household technology gadgets and appliances have an *effective impact* as they allow family members to expend less energy and effort. *This symbolises* the benefits in the time available as well as physical energy to complete other household tasks or leisure activities. For example, the use of slow cookers or electric coffee machines allows family members to be organised by cooking a meal while the family is at school/work/university/leisure or by programming the machine to start preparation at a certain time. This demonstrates the evidence that such household technology saves on cooking time and allows for multi-tasking.

In turn, this contributes to **positive wellbeing socially** as the family may have more time and energy available to spend together to enjoy each other's company through leisure and/or recreation thus contributing to family bonding. This also results in **improvements in wellbeing economically** as money is saved on pre-packaged foods and physically as foods that contain dangerous preservatives and additives are avoided, which will **impact on the overall health and wellbeing of the family**.

Conversely, household technology could have a *major undesirable impact* on interpersonal relationships through the division of labour and overuse/abuse. Household technology does save physical time and energy, but it often comes at an environmental cost through the high-energy consumption many of these appliances and gadgets expend. Coupled with the high costs of energy in today's society, such household technology may also place unwanted financial pressure on families. This in turn impacts on interpersonal relationships as families feel stress and tension as a result, which may then impact on their ability to be connect and support each other. This impacts on the family's **wellbeing emotionally, socially and economically** as the overuse of household technology may cause anxiety and conflict, which has resulted from possible high energy bills.

Entertainment technology as household technology also has a **substantial impact** on interpersonal relationships. The fun and enjoyment of using entertainment technology such as watching movies, listening to music and competing using game consoles can all create a sense of closeness and togetherness where families can enjoy being together and sharing special moments. These experiences can promote physical closeness, create an energetic atmosphere or a relaxing and happy atmosphere. *This in turn* could *impact positively* on other experiences as a family and lead to family members spending more time together. In addition, it may *contribute positively* to heighten their **wellbeing socially, as they feel like they belong, and emotionally,** as they have a positive self-esteem and self-concept where feelings of trust and understanding might foster due to the intimate family moment shared.

Negative impacts of entertainment technology on interpersonal family can surface as well. This may arise in the form of hostility, aggression, distractions, and decreased attention span. This can extend from explicit language, graphics, loud noises, flashes, animations and inappropriate themes presented through movies, reality television and online gaming. Entertainment technology may not be suited to the different ages of family members and often content is not suited to the viewer. *In addition*, many of these features can have a *detrimental effect* on brain processing and this may *impact* on communication in interpersonal family relationships. This could **impact on wellbeing physically,** through violence and abuse, **emotionally,** through inappropriate language leading to apprehension, distress and reduced self-esteem, and **socially,** in the breakdown of family communication leading to isolation, neglect and rejection.

Information and communication technology also has a *positive impact* on interpersonal family relationships. This is evident through the use of use of emailing, messaging and using social media to share news, stories, memories, photos and experiences with family members, especially those living remotely, interstate or overseas. Family members will feel a sense of connectedness and it may lead to positive bonds and enhanced communication as they are sharing these precious moments. This in turn *impacts* wellbeing **emotionally and socially** as family members will become closer as a family and be able to create memories together in the future.

Equally, there could be a *damaging impact* of technology on interpersonal relationships within families as it may lead families to develop unhealthy technology habits through the constant use of social media, inability to switch off due to around the clock accessibility, overreliance on the internet and the yearning to keep up with the latest developments and technology. This may have a *sizeable impact* on interpersonal relationships and stress, tension, anxiety and isolation may result. It may have a detrimental **impact on the wellbeing** of the family **socially** through a lack of connectedness and companionship, as well as **emotionally** through lowered self-esteem and tiredness.

Therefore, household technology, entertainment technology and information and communication technology can have both positive and negative impacts on interpersonal family relationships. Notably, there may be significant positive impacts through household technology and entertainment technology, and overwhelming negative impacts through the use of information and communication technology.

OR
Question 31 – Individuals and Work (25 marks)
(a) Outline the personal management skills required by youth in the workplace. (4 marks)

Personal management skills required by youth in the workplace *include the ability to* plan, organise, have open and clear communication, make decisions and problem solve.

Planning within a workplace may refer to planning of time by looking at their current and future rosters, projecting future budgets or planning how to use resources effectively. Successful planning involves being able to recognise what resources are available and how they can be used sustainably and/or be interchanged.

Planning can be difficult for young people as it requires looking ahead. Organisational skills *required by* youth may be related to attendance, punctuality, and organising files or stock.

Communications skills required in the workplace *relate to* clear, open communication. Young people will need to communicate with others around them. They may need to be assertive with their employer to ensure that they are not vulnerable to exploitation. An employer also will rely on youth in the workplace to make decisions and to problem solve. This will ensure that the workplace remains productive and time is not wasted.

(b) How does labour force participation vary across the life span? (6 marks)

The labour force is anyone who is considered either employed or unemployed (those ready and seeking employment). Labour force participation may vary across the life span *due to the* many circumstances an individual may face. Adolescence, the stage in the life span after childhood, sees the earliest phase of labour force participation in Australia. At this stage of life, young people are still involved in formal education such as school or TAFE, *and if they* enter the labour force they need flexibility in their work pattern to balance the demands of the two. Young people may leave school and enter into a full-time apprenticeship or traineeship, which will also involve a day of study, so their workplace will need to be flexible to allow the extra learning time.

After adolescence and moving into young adulthood will see similar labour force participation. Balancing work and study *may mean* young adults work part-time or casually, however it is usual that there is some labour force participation. This time *may also mean* a time of unemployment where young graduates leave university seeking employment in their career of choice. This may be difficult to find due to a lack of workplace-specific experience. *After this,* young adults may have established a career and be working to improve their adequate standard of living needs by seeking promotion. Women after this stage in adulthood may leave the workforce altogether or may seek flexible working patterns to help to support their new demands of motherhood. Males may continue to work to support their family and labour force participation will remain steady.

As individuals enter the aged stage of the life span at 65+ years, *many will have exited* the labour force, more so women than men. However, *if they are still participating* they may be seeking phased retirement, like many in the later stages of adulthood. Phased retirement means older workers *are still* working but at reduced hours or days.

(c) Assess how employees' rights and responsibilities are supported by workplace structures. (15 marks)

Every employee's rights will be supported by structures within the workplace. Rights relating to discrimination-free workplace, safe working environment, rates of pay and leave entitlements, practicing religion, equal opportunity and to join a union are met by workplaces creating structures to uphold these rights. With all rights, however, comes a moral obligation to fulfil the demands of that role in the manner expected by the employer. Structures that support these rights are: workplace legislation, working conditions, trade unions, flexible work patterns and practices, workplace culture and leave entitlements.

All employees have the right to receive payment for their work (unless stated otherwise through volunteer work patterns). They have the right to a clear rate of pay set out by the employer and it must be at least the minimum wage advised by the Fair Work Ombudsman. *This right is met* for employees through their industry-based award. Their working conditions or arrangements set out by the award states their rate of pay, any overtime they may be eligible for, rates of superannuation and any penalty rates they may receive. The award is industry based and the rates of pay will differ between industries such as the retail or telecommunications industry. Regardless of industry, all employees who have their right of payment, which is supported by the award, will have the responsibility to fulfil their duties set out by their employer. They must arrive to work on time, complete all set tasks with diligence and productively and work for the intended number of hours. Trade unions may also support employees' right to payment for the labour they provide. In cases where employees may not have been paid or received the correct payment, they may access grievance procedures and seek mediation from trade unions, which will fight on behalf of the employee and try to regain some of the missing money. It is an employee's right to join a trade union; however, employees have the responsibility to pay trade union fees for this support. The right to payment and having knowledge of a clear rate of pay will allow the employee to budget, prioritise their economic resources and allocate money to bills, their mortgage and to their adequate standard of living needs. Having knowledge of the rate of pay will ensure that economic factors will not influence the wellbeing of the employee. Being supported by a step-by-step process that a grievance procedure provides and a trade union will limit the emotional factors of stress and create peace of mind, influencing the employees' overall wellbeing.

Employees have the right to a safe working environment. This means that employees upon entering the workplace have knowledge of the risks and procedures to eliminate harms from these risks. *This right will only be met if* the workplace follows legislation. The *Work Health and Safety Act 2011* aims to protect the health and safety of all employees by supporting their rights. Employees' rights *are fully supported* by this legislation's creation of clear processes and procedures for all tasks to eliminate or reduce risk. The legislation ensures that all employees have access to training and protective equipment, for example when a new apprentice enters a worksite they will be put through safety induction training, such as the white card. They will be issued with protective helmets and must have appropriate footwear. When training courses are offered and protective equipment is issued, employees have the responsibility to use the equipment and follow all procedures taught in the training. They have the responsibility to ensure their behaviour does not impact on the safety of those around them and to report any conduct that does not align with WHS laws. When an employee is kept safe and provided with the knowledge and equipment to keep safe, there is less likely to be injury or illness within the workplace, ensuring that these physical factors do not cause ill-being.

Employees have the right to a workplace free from discrimination and harassment, where they are protected from unfair dismissal and given the right to equal opportunity within the workplace, and thus have the opportunity to seek, find and be promoted. This right is *supported by* legislation such as the Equal Employment Opportunity Act. This workplace structure set out by the government aims to create the best, most supportive working environment while ensuring the best, most qualified person gains employment regardless of their gender, marital status, sexuality, culture or religion. This legislation *also aims to* remove prejudices when employees go for promotion or seek a training course. These rights will also be supported by the workplace culture. To create equality and allow employees to meet their right of practicing religion, a supportive workplace culture *would create* a space for a non-denominational prayer room – a quiet space to practice religion when needed. If employees have these entitlements, *which are highly supported* by workplace structures, then they have the moral obligation (responsibility) to eliminate all prejudice behaviour, use open communication to address everyone in fair and supportive/inclusive language, use prayer rooms at appropriate times and not abuse the space or time given.

When employees feel supported despite their diversity, they are more likely to have peace of mind and reduce emotional factors such as stress and conflict from their working lives, positively influencing their wellbeing.

Workplace structures are designed and have been created to support the rights of employees within the workplace. It is a moral obligation for employees to meet their roles and duties set out by these rights and support structures.

****If space and time allow, this candidate could also discuss the right to access leave entitlements, which are supported by the leave entitlements set out by their Award or their working agreement.